Printing Colors in Graphic Design

CMYK & PMS

SP
SendPoints

Printing Colors in Graphic Design
CMYK & PMS

© 2016 SendPoints Publishing Co., Ltd.

EDITED & PUBLISHED BY SendPoints Publishing Co., Ltd.

PUBLISHER: Lin Gengli

PUBLISHING DIRECTOR: Lin Shijian

CHIEF EDITOR: Lin Shijian

EXECUTIVE EDITOR: Huang Shaojun

ART DIRECTOR: He Wanling

EXECUTIVE ART EDITOR: Lok Hoi Yan

PROOFREADING: Huang Shaojun & Jeff Karon

REGISTERED ADDRESS: Room 15A Block 9 Tsui Chuk Garden, Wong Tai Sin, Kowloon, Hong Kong

TEL: +852-35832323 / **FAX:** +852-35832448

OFFICE ADDRESS: 7F, 9th Anning Street, Jinshazhou, Baiyun District, Guangzhou, China

TEL: +86-20-89095121 / **FAX:** +86-20-89095206

BEIJING OFFICE: Room 107, Floor 1, Xiyingfang Alley, Ande Road, Dongcheng District, Beijing, China

TEL: +86-10-84139071 / **FAX:** +86-10-84139071

SHANGHAI OFFICE: Room 307, Building 1, Hong Qiang Creative, Zhabei District, Shanghai, China

TEL: +86-21-63523469 / **FAX:** +86-21-63523469

SALES MANAGER: Sissi

TEL: +86-20-81007895

EMAIL: overseas01@sendpoints.cn

WEBSITE: www.sendpoints.cn / www.spbooks.cn

ISBN 978-988-14704-2-3

Printed and bound in China.

WHAT
IS
CMYK

According to the science of color, the color black absorbs all wavelengths while white reflects all wavelengths. When an object is illuminated, it absorbs and reflects different parts of the spectrum. The part of the spectrum that is not absorbed and remains visible is the object's color that we perceive, which is known as a color subtracting process. This way of perceiving colors is applied in the printing industry by developing a CMYK color model (process color or four color) which can greatly reproduce the colors in our world.

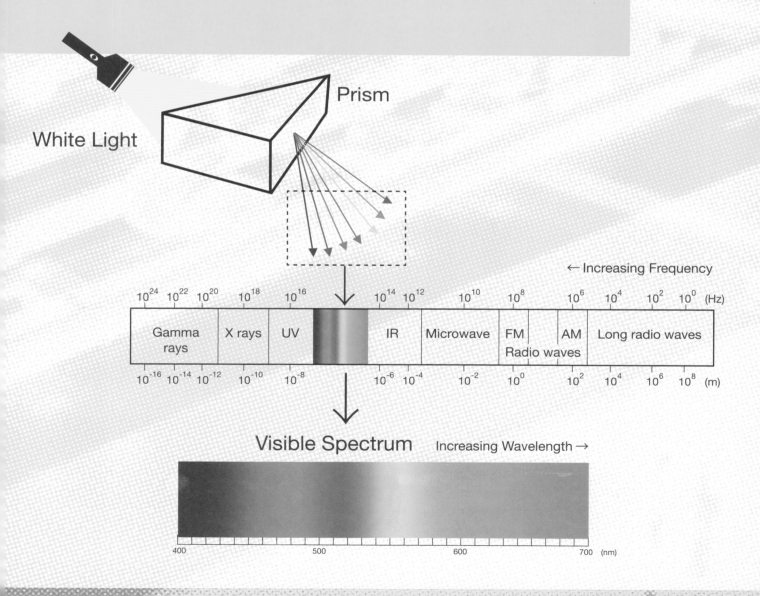

Prism

White Light

← Increasing Frequency

10^{24} 10^{22} 10^{20} 10^{18} 10^{16} 10^{14} 10^{12} 10^{10} 10^{8} 10^{6} 10^{4} 10^{2} 10^{0} (Hz)

| Gamma rays | X rays | UV | | IR | Microwave | FM | AM | Long radio waves |

Radio waves

10^{-16} 10^{-14} 10^{-12} 10^{-10} 10^{-8} 10^{-6} 10^{-4} 10^{-2} 10^{0} 10^{2} 10^{4} 10^{6} 10^{8} (m)

Visible Spectrum   Increasing Wavelength →

400   500   600   700 (nm)

CMYK refers to four inks: cyan, magenta, yellow, and key (black). Based on the theory of three primary colors, the CMYK color model mixes the four pigments in varying amounts to produce a wide range of colors. There are two main reasons for adding key (black) to the primary colors: (1) the quality of "black" generated by mixing just commercially practical cyan, magenta, and yellow inks is unsatisfactory since doing so generates dark grey; and (2) it is cheaper to use a separate black ink instead of combining the three colored inks. Thus the addition of black ink makes it possible to properly darken areas as needed while reducing printing costs which is why this four-color printing method is the most widely used in the printing industry.

 C: 100%
M:0%
Y: 0%
K: 0%

 C: 0%
M:100%
Y: 0%
K: 0%

K: 100%

 C: 0%
M:0%
Y: 100%
K: 0%

 C: 0%
M:0%
Y: 0%
K: 100%

K: 100% C: 30%

If the separate black ink, K100, fails to generate desirable black areas, try to combine K100, C30 or K100, C50, M50 to achieve a darker result.

K: 100% C: 50% M: 50%

THE REPRODUCTION OF COLORS

Four-color presses are the most extensively used presses in the printing industry today. Each four-color press is equipped with four rollers. The pigments on the rollers are mixed to reproduce desired colors.

Heidelberg Four-Color Printing Press View from Right of Four-Color Printing Press Machine

Four-Color Printing Press Machine Roller with Blue Ink

Four-Color Printing Press Machine Roller with Red Ink

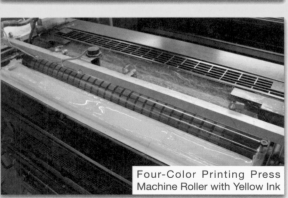

Four-Color Printing Press Machine Roller with Yellow Ink

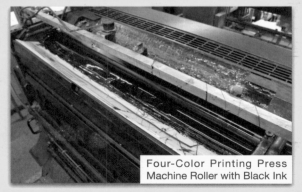

Four-Color Printing Press Machine Roller with Black Ink

Under the CMYK color model, the printed material is separated into four color plates—red, green, blue, and black—which is called color separations. These four printing plates would be aligned to reproduce the printing matter's original color. The platemaking is very important because the type of screening, screen density, and the size and shape of dots must be determined during this process.

CMYK Separations

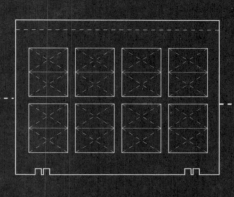

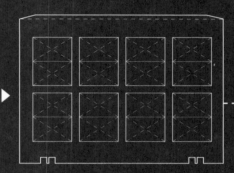

Cutting the Plates to Fit for the Printing Press Machine

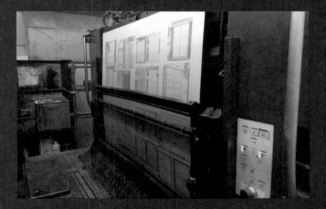

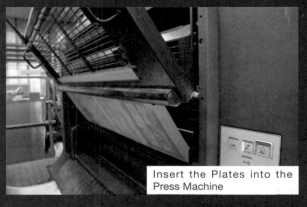

Insert the Plates into the Press Machine

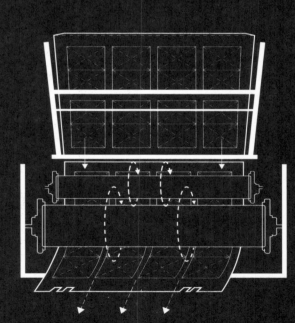

FM SCREENING
AND
AM SCREENING

Screening is the process after rasterizing PDF files in the RIP (raster image processor) during prepress. There are two main screening types, FM screening (Frequency Modulation Screening) and AM screening (Amplitude Modulation Screening).

FM screening or stochastic screening is based on size-fixed dots and a distribution density to create different tones—low-density for bright tones and high-density for the darker. This means that there is no need to consider screen angles. And printers can use more than four plates for a finer reproduction of the original colors of the printed materials without worrying about misregistration as FM screening eliminates this problem. But the tiny dot size used in FM screening creates difficulties in proofing and platemaking.

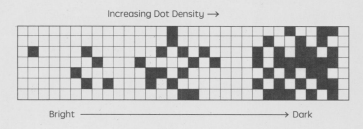

Increasing Dot Density →

Bright ————————————→ Dark

AM screening is more popular than FM screening due to its long history. As opposed to FM screening, it is characterized by a consistent distribution density and creates different tones by varying the dot size. The size, shape, and angle of dots and LPI (halftone frequency) should be taken into consideration when this screening method is chosen.

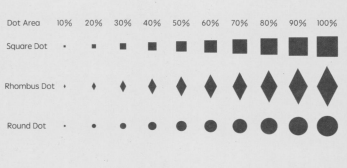

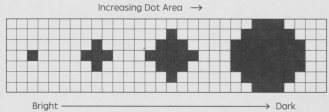

Increasing Dot Area →

Bright ————————————→ Dark

HALFTONE
DOTS
/
SCREENING
DOTS

In practice, CMYK separations are interpreted as tiny dots varying in size and spacing. In other words, the printed materials are actually in the form of dots in a regular pattern or matrix. Different size and spacing of the dots create different hue, value, and saturation, which greatly affect the printing result.

DOT

SIZE

The dot size of a halftone is expressed as a percentage of the total surface area, which can range from 0% (no dot) to 100% (solid ink density). There are two ways to measure the dot area. One is to use a densitometer. The other is to make a rough computation with a magnifier, which is convenient but requires extensive experience. To identify the dot area within 50% depends on the number of dots held by the space between two dots on the vertical or horizontal dotted line.

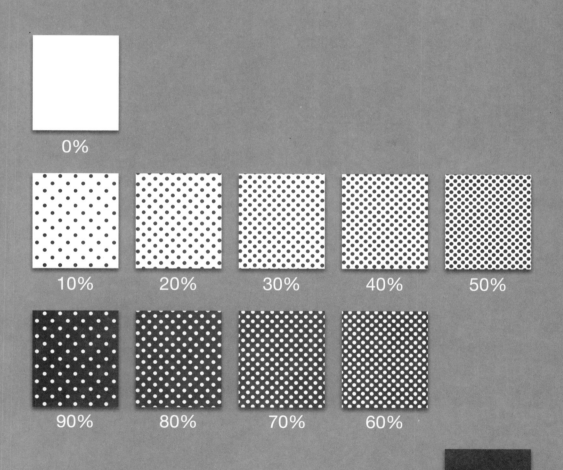

0%

10%   20%   30%   40%   50%

90%   80%   70%   60%

100%

Dot Area under a Magnifier

K10

If the space can hold three dots of the same size, the dot area density reaches 10%.

K20

If the space can hold two dots of the same size, the dot area density reaches 20%.

K30

If the space can hold 1.5 dots of the same size, the dot area density reaches 30%.

If the space can hold 1.25 dots of the same size, the dot area density reaches 40%.

If the space can only hold one dot of the same size—that is, the black area is equal to the white one—the dot area density reaches 50%.

The dot areas above 50% are correspondingly opposite to the ones below 50%. In other words, a 10% dot area plus a 90% dot area is solid ink density. The interconversion of the black dots and the white part of a 40% dot area can produce a 60% dot area, and 30% produce a 70%. The rest can be done in the same manner. The higher the dot area density is, the darker the printing matter looks. The lower the dot area density is, the lighter the printing matter looks. There are three grades of tone: highlights, midtones, and shadows. Highlights usually match a density ranging from 10% to 30%, midtones 40% to 60%, and shadows 70% to 90%.

DOT
SHAPE

Dot shape refers to the shape of an individual dot. There are different dot shapes available, each of them having their own characteristics. The most common are round, square, elliptical, and rhombus. Applied in different ways, they create various printing effects and quality. But under the condition of a 50% dot area, the most popular shapes are square, round, and rhombus. Under the condition of a 50% dot area, square dots featuring sharp shapes would create a checkered-like pattern that yields a strong sense of layering.

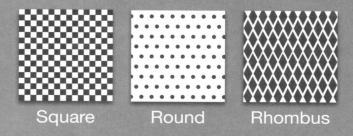

Square   Round   Rhombus

Round dots, whether under the condition of highlights or midtones, are independent of one another. Even the condition of shadows can only make a part of them connected. It is hard to create a satisfactory sense of layering when this dot shape is used. Therefore, round dots are rarely used for four-color printing. Combining the "tough" characteristic of square dots and the "gentle" characteristic of round dots, rhombus dots reproduce smooth gradients.

SCREEN
ANGLE

During the platemaking, the correct sets of screen angles are very important as incorrect sets of angle values lead to undesirable Moiré patterns. The commonly used screen angles are 90°, 75°, 45°, and 15°. According to experience and theory, the least visible color, yellow, is placed at the most visible angle 0° (90°) while the most visible color, black, is placed at 45°. The cyan and magenta are then placed between these two, cyan at 15° (105°) and magenta at 75°. This reasonable arrangement helps avoid Moiré patterns.

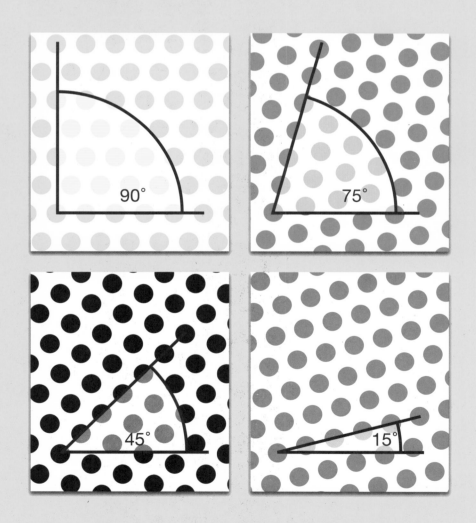

LINES
PER
INCH
(LPI)

Analogous to DPI, lines per inch (LPI) is a measurement of the halftone resolution. High LPI indicates greater details and sharpness of the printing result which is also affected by the type of paper and the quality of ink.

A 300 DPI bitmap image, as we know, is an image consisting of 300 pixels per inch. But you can find that it is actually made up of many tiny dots at various sizes when enlarging it. Generally, the dots are packed in a regular pattern and form dotted lines. We express the number of lines formed by the tiny dots in a vertically or horizontally linear inch as Line/Inch, abbreviated as LPI, which is also referred to as halftone frequency. 150 LPI, for example, means there are 150 halftone lines printed in a linear inch.

Specific LPI ranges as below are commonly used for various printing qualities by the printing industry: 10-120 LPI cannot generate quality results but is fit for large printing matters, such as newspapers, and posters and ads that can be seen from a distance. 150 LPI is usually required by a CMYK printing code. 175-200 LPI allow fine printing quality. 250-300 LPI guarantee a higher one if needed.

Projects

Food for Thought

Some books are just books and some are "Food for Thought." This is the packaging concept for three limited edition books (*Breakfast at Tiffany's, Naked Lunch* and *Dinner at the Homesick Restaurant*). These inspiring novels with edible names encourage profound thinking. The labels were colored to mimic traditional food cans, echoing the theme of "Food for Thought."

CMYK

Design: Maria Mordvintseva-Keeler

EIGHT MARTINIS BEFORE DINNER

100 PER CENT NAKED

SALLY

ACCIDENTS happen

Scar RESTA

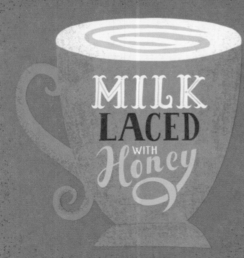

MILK LACED WITH Honey

CR CASS

Finest
BRANDY
100
YEARS OLD

100 PER CENT
CONSOLING

You're OLD
FOR SO MUCH LONGER
than you're
YOUNG
Really it
HARDLY
seems fair

PEARL TULL

ANNE
TYLER
1982
DINNER
AT THE HOMESICK
RESTAURANT
a novel
300
PAGES

It's better
TO LOOK
at the SKY
THAN live
THERE

TRUMAN
CAPOTE
1958
BREAKFAST
AT TIFFANY'S
a short novel and
three stories
160
PAGES

Holly Golightly

Ars Cameralis Festival 2015

The 24th Ars Cameralis Festival is a multi-disciplinary celebration of visual arts, music, literature and theatre. Its participants should create his or her own personal collection at the time of choosing the event in which they wish to participate. Marta Gawin created two unique animals, namely unicorn and rhinoceros which are reworked to correspond to the colorful Gothic stained glass, medieval manuscripts and ancient mosaics in terms of color palette and style. The aim was to convey a fairy-tale, dreamlike atmosphere and the wealth of experience provided by the event.

Design: Marta Gawin

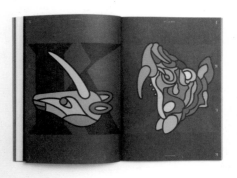

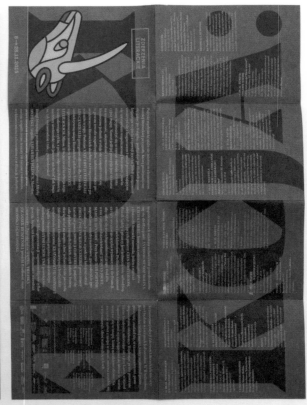

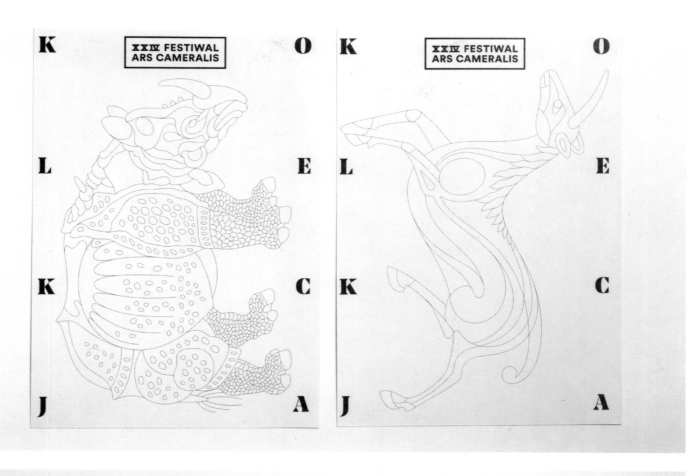

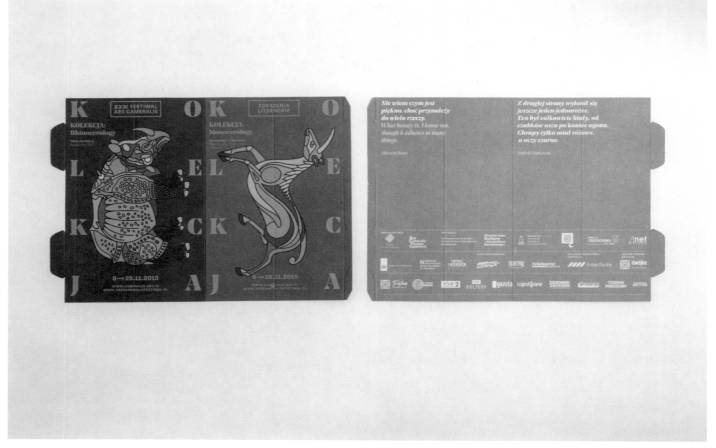

Le Théâtre des Bouffes du Nord

Le Théâtre des Bouffes du Nord is a Parisian theater. Its general theme for the 2015/2016 season is "COLOR." The designer used abstract splashes of ink and playful watercolor to echo the theme, translating the global feeling of the whole season in a visual way.

CMYK

Design: Violaine & Jérémy

THEÂTRE
DES BOUFFES
DU NORD

saison
2015 —— 2016

oct.
——
nov.

10ᵉ——15ᵉ
ADESSO
VOGLIO MUSICA
E BASTA

Voyage à travers le monde
musical de Pippo Delbono

11ᵉ——17ᵉ
MIES JULIE

D'après Mademoiselle Julie d'August Strindberg

Yaël Farber

10ᵉ
IMOGEN COOPER

12ᵉ
STÉPHANE DEGOUT
ET ALAIN PLANÈS

THEÂTRE
DES BOUFFES
DU NORD

saison
2015 —— 2016

avril
——
mai

10ᵉ——14ᵉ
ARCHIPEL
MARIE NDIAYE

Marie NDiaye
Georges Lavaudant

15ᵉ——17ᵉ
VERSO MEDEA

Spectaculairement d'après Euripide

Emma Dante

16ᵉ
THOMAS ENHCO ET
VASSILENA SERAFIMOVA

12ᵉ
DELPHINE HAIDAN
ENSEMBLE APPASSIONATO
MATHIEU HERZOG

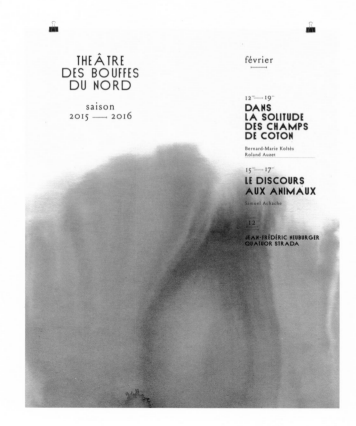

THEÂTRE
DES BOUFFES
DU NORD

saison
2015 —— 2016

février
——→

12ᵉ——19ᵉ
DANS
LA SOLITUDE
DES CHAMPS
DE COTON

Bernard-Marie Koltès
Roland Auzet

15ᵉ——17ᵉ
LE DISCOURS
AUX ANIMAUX

Samuel Achache

12
JEAN-FRÉDÉRIC NEUBURGER
QUATUOR STRADA

Wrapping Paper

Knot for, Inc. designed the wrapping paper based on the theme of "Time for Tea." There are two types of packaging: white-based and black-based. The former is acrylic painting filled with motifs of tea sets and tableware such as teapot and spoon while the latter presents geometric patterns of candy, cake, teapot and spoon. The repeating colorful patterns depict a dreamy tone as well as a playful sense.

Design: Knot for, Inc.

Mochiice New Concept

The design team created a take-away package for Mochiice to attract the Swedish market. Irregular patterns and vivid colors are used to enhance the colorful confections and make the brand appeal to the young customers.

Design: Jessica Sjöstedt, Natasha Frolova, Louise Olofsson

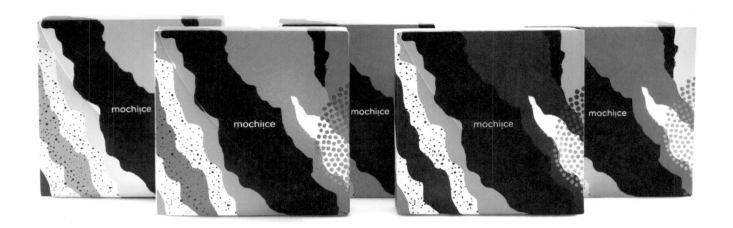

Snežana Pupović's Business Card

This series of illustrated business cards was printed on uncoated cardboard in bright colors. The colored parts were emphasized with a pale grey background.

PUPOVIĆ
SNEŽANA

artist, graphic designer

067 390 578
snezapupovic@yahoo.com

Design: Snežana Pupović

PUPOVIĆ
SNEZANA

artist, graphic designer

067 390 578
snezapupovic@yahoo.com

Black Condor Pomade

Black Condor is a brand of haircare products that caters to the Rockabilly lifestyle of 1950's Americana. Its packaging design intends to be vintage yet modern and makes the brand stand out on store shelves amongst other pomade brands. The boxes were created in a matchbox style to represent the retro vibe of a greaser lighting his cigarette with a match. The varnish pattern on the sides of the bow represents the thick immovable pompadours Rockabilly men would wear during this era. The silhouette of a condor was used uniformly throughout the products in an eye catching blue and orange with overlays.

Design: Kevin Craft

tre·tea

Packaging design for tre·tea, a tea brand.
"Tre" means "three" in Italian. The tea box therefore was designed
as a triangular prism. Each of the three birds on the sides figuratively
represent a flavor: the white bird represents white tea, the black bird
represents black tea and colorful bird represents tropical tea.

CMYK

Design: Natalia Bivol

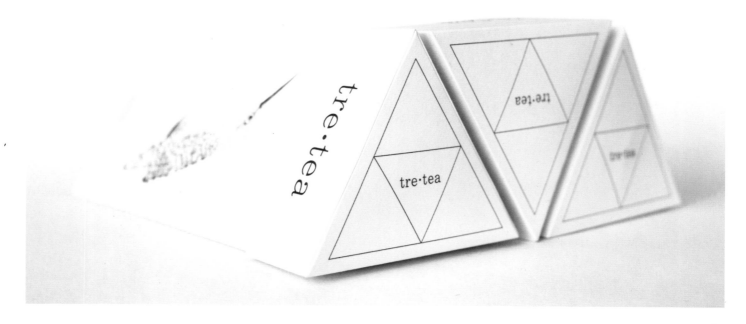

The Rose Bud

Poster design for The Rose Bud, a dance performance.

The poster, also serving as an invitation letter, is beautifully made by hand. Using the delicate traditional Chinese paper (Shuen paper) shows Chinese grace and charm. Being printed in a pure rosy color highlights the theme, "In the Name of the Rose."

Design: Zhang Yazhou & Huang Shu

Hornhuset

Visual Identity for Hornhuset, a restaurant.
Hornhuset is like a bustling, little square in Stockholm, Sweden. It's a wonderful place for those who want to enjoy a menu of flavorful, smaller dishes, or buy exceptionally tasty takeout. In order to convey a Mediterranean atmosphere for Hornhuset, Under uses fresh, bold colors such as ocean blue, bright yellow and ivory white that create a sunshine beach feeling.

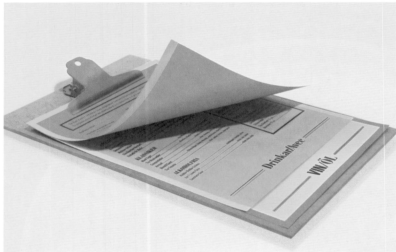

Design: Under

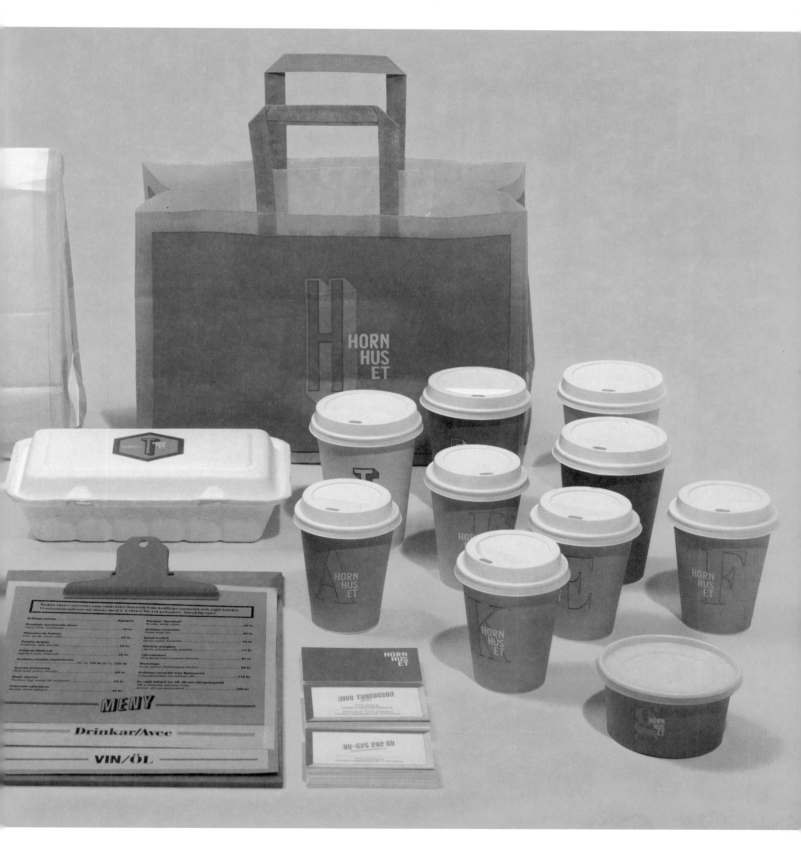

SKÖRDEFEST!
SVERIGE VS ITALIEN
26
TILL
28
SEPTEMBER
PÅ TORGET & KROGEN
WORKSHOPS
—
TORSDAG & FREDAG
NY MENY!
Rapsgris, lamm, färska svenska nötter och säsongens grönsaker
MARMELAD-KOKNING!
KORVFABRIK LIVE PÅ TORGET!
VAR? Långholmsgatan 15B, Hornstull
HEMSIDA www.hornhuset.se
RING 08-525 202 60
HORN HUS ET

SKALDJURS-DAGAR

Hornhuset slår upp dörrarna klockan 10.00 alla dagar i veckan och håller öppet ända in på småtimmarna. Som ett stimmigt litet torg någonstans runt Medelhavet, en smältdegel för de som vill njuta av en bit mat, träffa folk eller köpa riktigt bra take-out.

FREDAGEN 23/11 KL 18–23

HORN HUS ET

VAR? Långholmsgatan 15B, Hornstull HEMSIDA www.hornhuset.se RING 08-525 202 60

Moley Talhaoui
01.04 – 02.05.2013

Bus int, quuntion conseru menti
audicae. Us erunt. Renimporion
verferest quisimus, offictatiam
Quia paritaspe ellabor re pa p
arupiciis as dolorrorem. Quia

...ADO FRÅN SPANIEN
...TAVLA
...FOTAD GRIS IBERICO PÚRO

OKTO...

- SHERRY
- KORVAR
- CHORIZO
- LOMO
- VINO TINTO

ITE BLAND ANNAT:

Qoniki Brand Identity

Qoniki is an urban multi-brand sneaker and apparel store for kids. It needs a fun, cool and hip branding that would appeal to kids ranging from 5-12 years old and differ from other brands. The shield logo and different icons were created such as the Bad Teddy and Rebel Rabbit to underline the rebellious side of kids.

Design: Ipek Eris Design

Aleris

Aleris is one of Scandinavia's leading private healthcare companies. The company wants a new visual identity to increase brand awareness and to make Aleris an attractive choice to its target audience. The new visual identity is based on health and wellbeing. The new logotype was inspired by tree rings which symbolize growth, life and the care Aleris provides. The main color turquoise working with other refreshing colors expresses a warm and friendly message to its audience. It also gives a feeling of serenity and stability.

CMYK

Inspiration

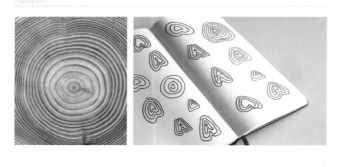

Typeface and colour palette

Logotype

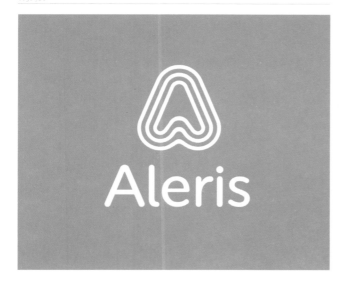

Pictograms

Design: Bold Scandinavia

2Day Languages

Masquespacio designed the identity and the interior for 2Day Languages, a new Spanish school in Valencia. The overall design was based on a three-tone color palette, which presents the three levels A, B, and C, established by the Common European Framework of Reference for Languages, here seen as the colors blue, yellow, and pink. The gradient color, by contrast, symbolized the process of language learning.

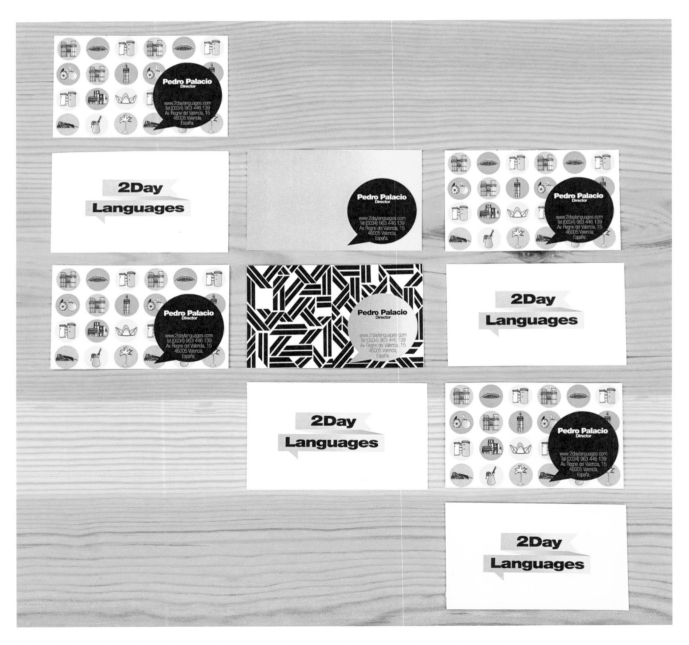

Design: Ana Milena Hernández Palacios (Masquespacio) / Photo: David Rodríguez from Cualiti

Handmade Business Card

Business Card for Matheus Dacosta, an artist and designer.
The artistic card series unifies his work in visual arts and design. Each one
is unique with a special pattern and color design.

Design: Matheus Dacosta

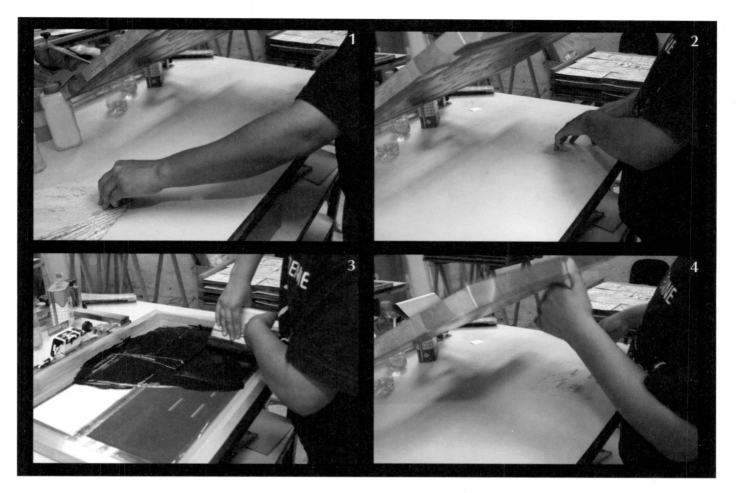

Print All Over Me Collaboration

An artwork for Print All Over Me (PAOM).
Print All Over Me is an online platform for real-world collaboration and creation. It provides the tools that allow anyone to create, share, own, and produce their designs by uploading artwork that can be applied to seasonal collections of clothing and objects. This project is full of strong color contrasts. Cool colors and warm colors were placed together to create a bright and fashionable result.

Design: Leta Sobierajski

MUD Identity

Short for Making Upward Dance, MUD Centro Danza is a dance school in Italy.
The identity was designed to express the two complementary characters behind the scenes:
the founders Silvia and Leonardo. The two-color palettes were used to reflect this.

Design: The Clocksmiths

Sommerfest 2013

Orange, a warm color chosen as the dominant hue for the identity design, forms a very strong contrast to the complementary white, grey and black and meanwhile adds a lively atmosphere for a summer party focusing on visual design and illustration.

CMYK

Design: Daniel Brokstad

Queen Muar's Money Packet

Queen Muar is a home-based festival cookie bakery in southern Malaysia. This series of money packets was designed for Queen Muar to capture their customers' attention with new style and color combinations that rarely can be found on traditional money packets. The bold colors, flower patterns and golden " 福 "(A Chinese character meaning good fortune) create a strong Asian-style New Year atmosphere.

CMYK

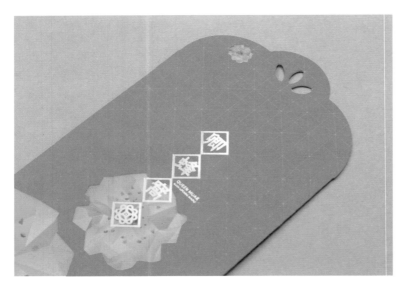

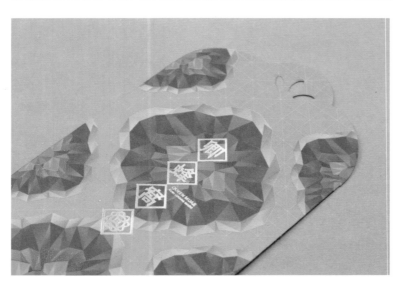

Design: AT HOME CREATIVE

Six & Five Branding Identity

Six & Five is a contemporary art studio exploring the frontier zone between art and design. The bright tone injects uniqueness and purity into the brand and presents an energetic image.

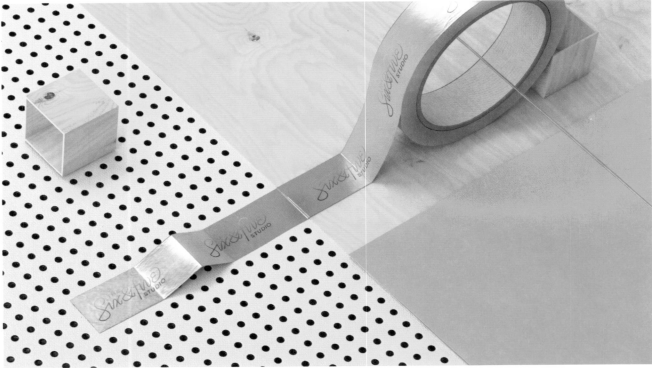

Six & Five Branding Identity

Design: Six & Five Studio

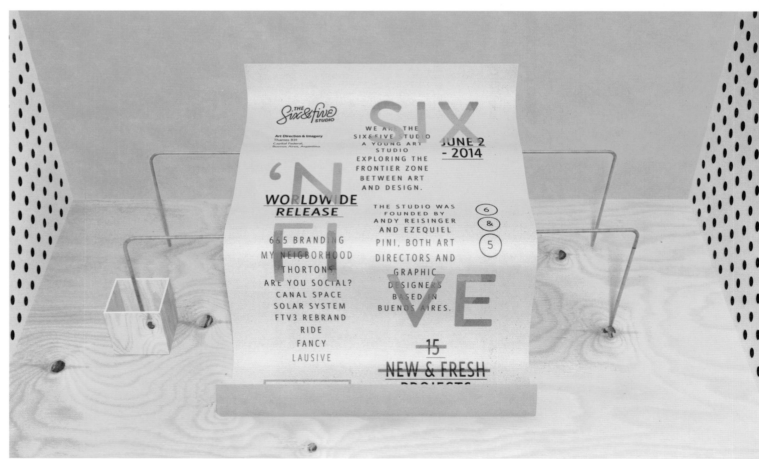

Kinetica

Kinetica is an ingenious industrial design bureau offering custom solutions for non-standard architectural challenges. Its identity was based on the simple concept of modular grids with movement. The only generic and geometric shape is a circle. Modern design, bright color, Swiss typography and grids create an industrial yet classy atmosphere.

CMYK

Design: Face

Biografias Vimaranenses

This is a series of biographical books about 12 historical figures from the city of Guimarães, Portugal. Visually, they are faux-traditional books in the way they use an old-style graphical treatment combined with a non-standard structure to display the notes. The contemporary touch also comes from the fluorescent pink that highlights the typography. Geometric compositions were added to each cover, made directly through the overlaying of different silkscreen prints.

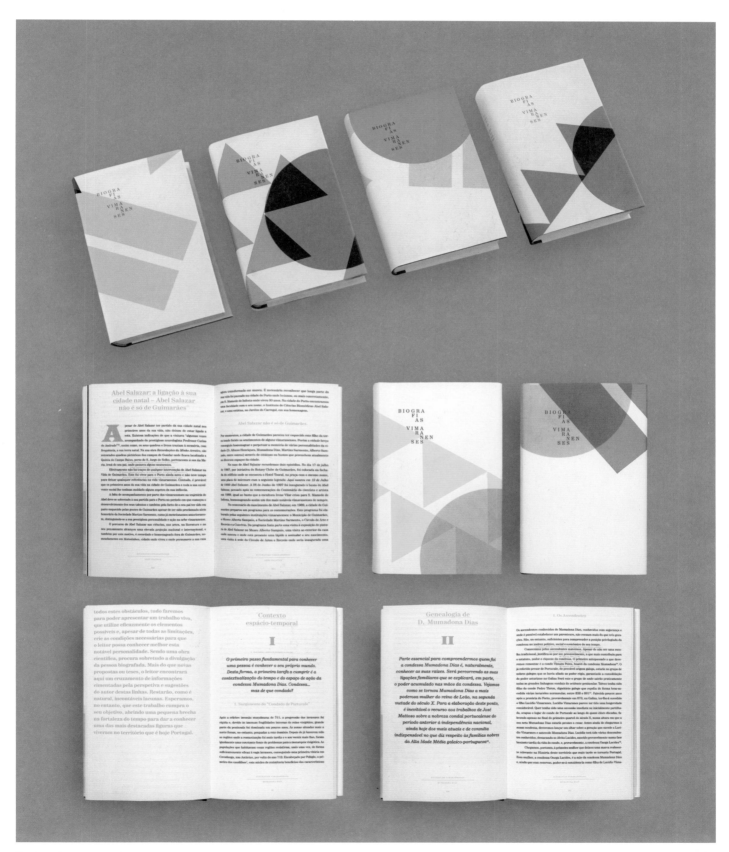

Design: Non Verbal Club

Music Album by Susu

An illustrated CD album, 冥明 , for a young music artist from China, Su Yun Ying (Susu).
An illustration of wild fantasy, imaginative nature is the core design of the album that reflects the personality of Susu as a creative, imaginative and energetic person who enjoys music. Rich colors help to create a vivid illustration and also match the color palette of the disk, blue and yellow.

Design: Magdalene Wong

Illumination

Album design for Illumination, an album including 10 singers (contestants of Sing My Song, a Chinese television program).
Ten types of "light" in different forms and colors were designed for the ten singers and then printed on cards. On the backs
of the cards display the lyrics of the songs sung by the singers. Each card could be the cover of the album.

CMYK

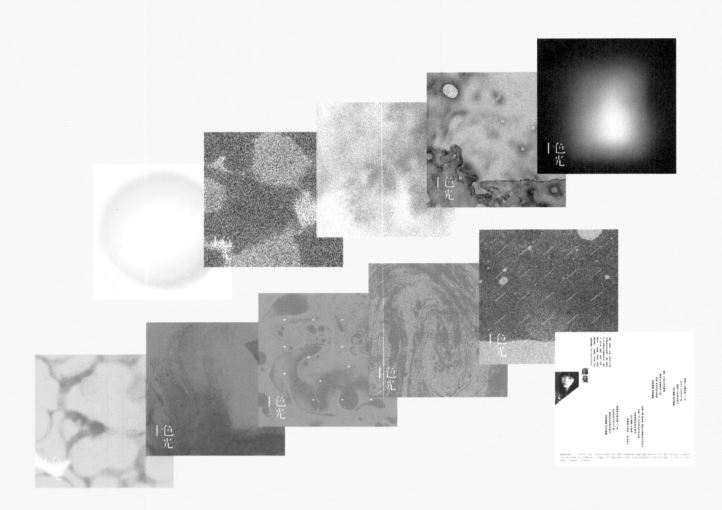

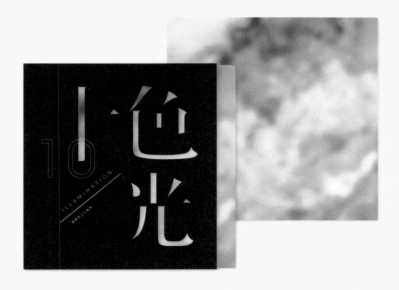

Design: Magdalene Wong

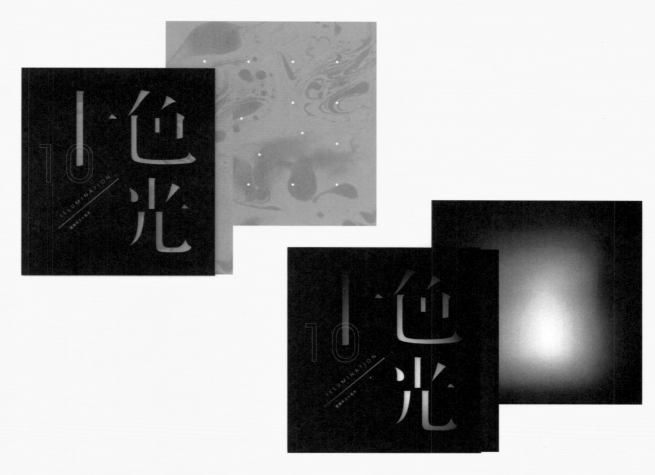

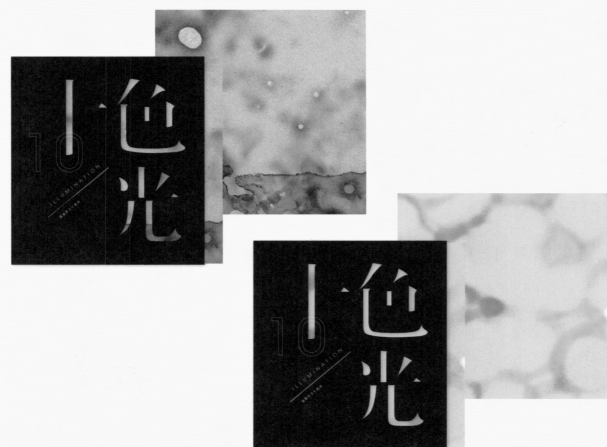

Novelty Identity

Novelty is a boutique that sells casual apparel to young women with a taste for fresh, modern fashion. The pink color expresses a strong feminine identity while the watercolor marks on the stationery and the collage-like composition of its printed ad add a sense of fashion.

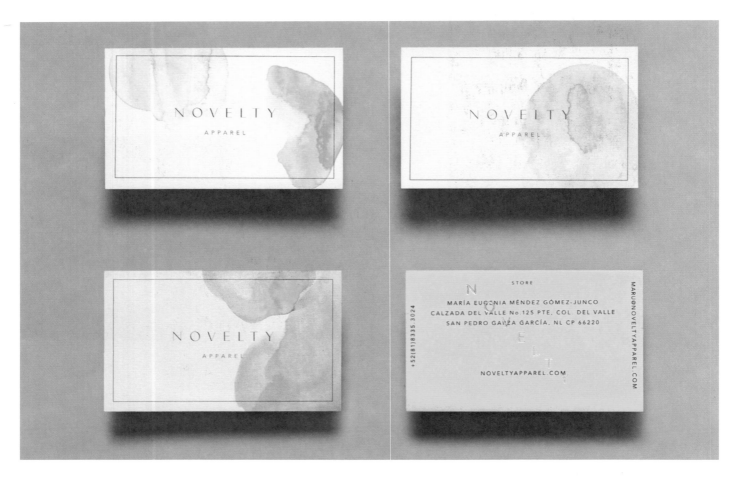

STORE
N
MARÍA EUGENIA MÉNDEZ GÓMEZ-JUNCO
CALZADA DEL VALLE No.125 PTE, COL. DEL VALLE
SAN PEDRO GARZA GARCÍA, NL CP 66220

+52(81)8335.3024

MARU@NOVELTYAPPAREL.COM

E
L
T

NOVELTYAPPAREL.COM

Design: Anagrama

APPAREL

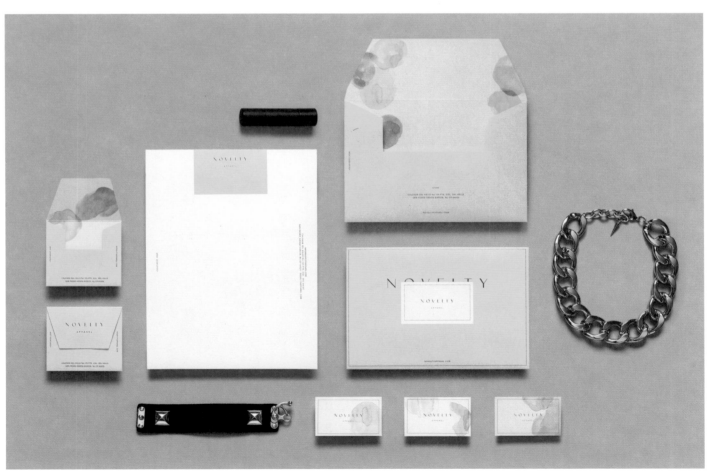

Eden

Saburo Sakata designs the package for eden, a confectionery store located in Yamada train station. To convey the deliciousness of candies and pastries, Sakata rearranges the colors of Ai Sasaki's drawing with delicate pastel colors. By printing on paper, the design turns out to be a gift package in a dreamy and colorful tone.

Design: Saburo Sakata

Popular Lies about Graphic Design

Written by Craig Ward, *Popular Lies about Graphic Design* is in an attempt to debunk the various misconceptions, half-truths and, in some cases, outright lies which permeate the industry of design. The book is small and printed in double black on a tactile, uncoated stock. The center pages, featuring contributions from other designers such as David Carson, Milton Glaser and many others, are printed on a fluorescent orange stock. White Futura typeface against the solid black cover·highlights the book title.

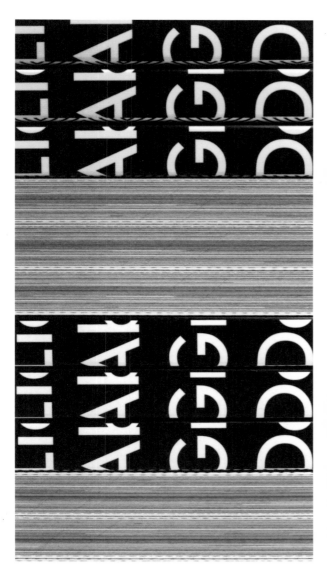

CMYK

Design: Craig Ward

CEE Identity

Coalition for Engaged Education is an LA-based organization that helps vulnerable children and young adults realize their potential through an approach to education that respects and inspires them. This new identity was designed to express the organization's new goal at a national level. CEE's enthusiasm is reflected in the choice of language throughout the design. The stationery and posters are unified by a broad color palette and uncoated paper while a complementary color palette was chosen for the stickers. The rich hues contribute to a young and dynamic brand.

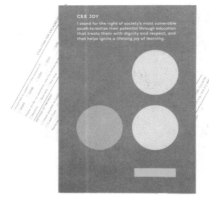

Design: Blok Design

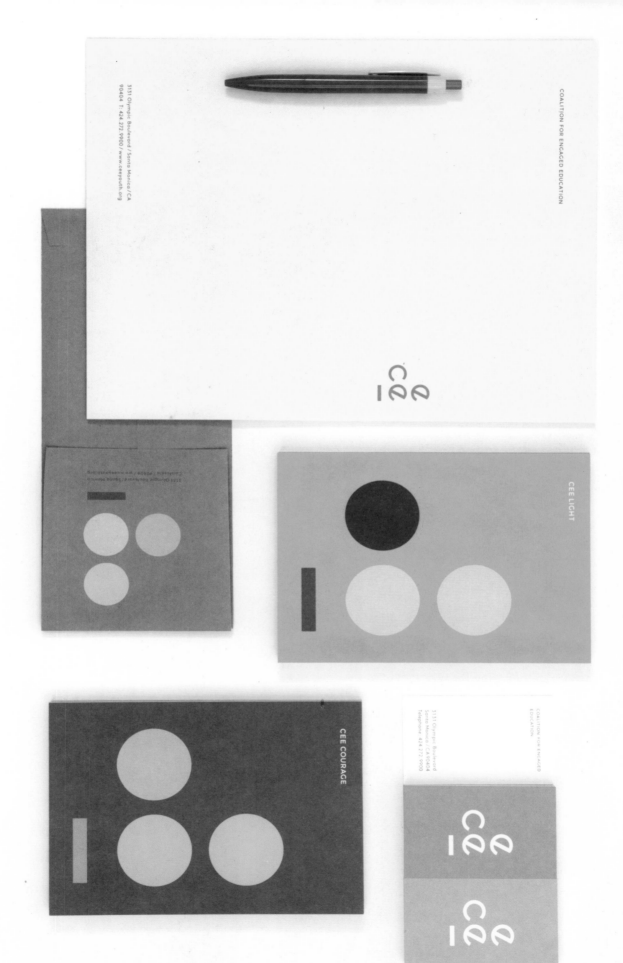

The Swedish History Museum

Visual Identity for the Swedish History Museum.
The new identity should arouse curiosity and interest in Swedish history and revitalise the museum. So the designers chose a red color appearing all over the visual identity to make an active and dynamic impression. In addition, consisting of a classic serif font and a modern sans-serif font, the new logo could be used in varying forms. Its left part can be replaced with historical artifacts and the color of the right part keeps changing, which highlights the objects and stories the museum offers and endows a playful feature for the museum.

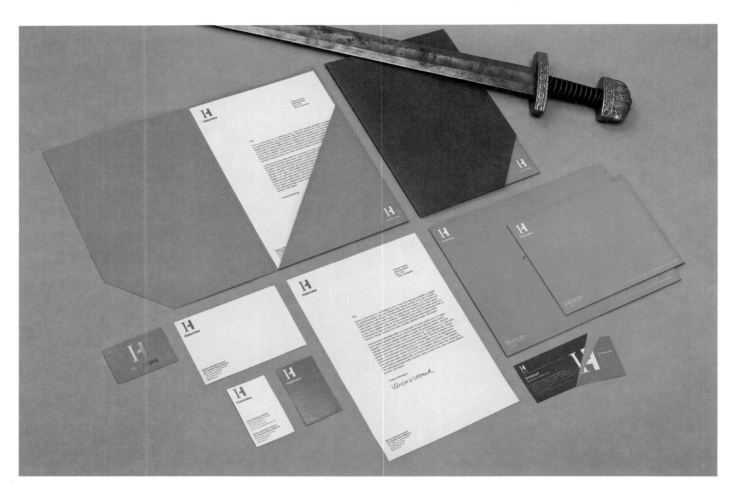

Design: Bold Scandinavia

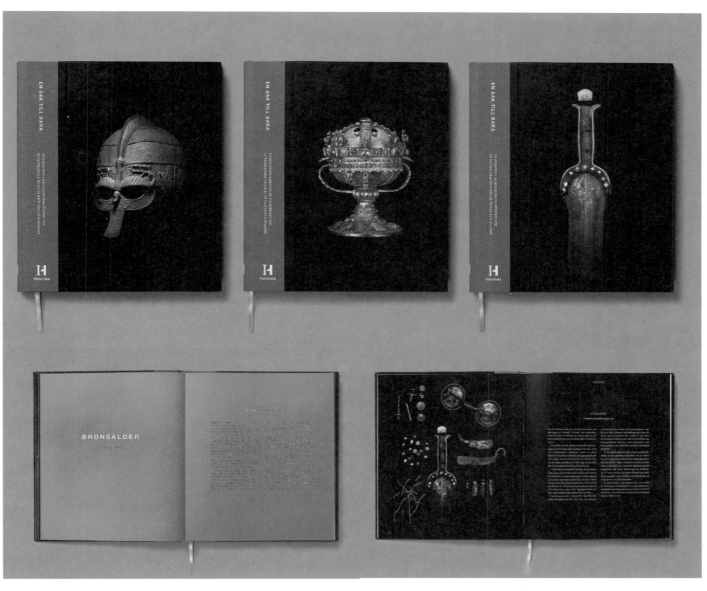

SSU

Branding identity for Sweden's Social Democratic Youth League (SSU).
The visual identity of SSU is based on a red/white color palette. The dominant red color
brightens the identity and creates a passionate and bold impression for the organization.

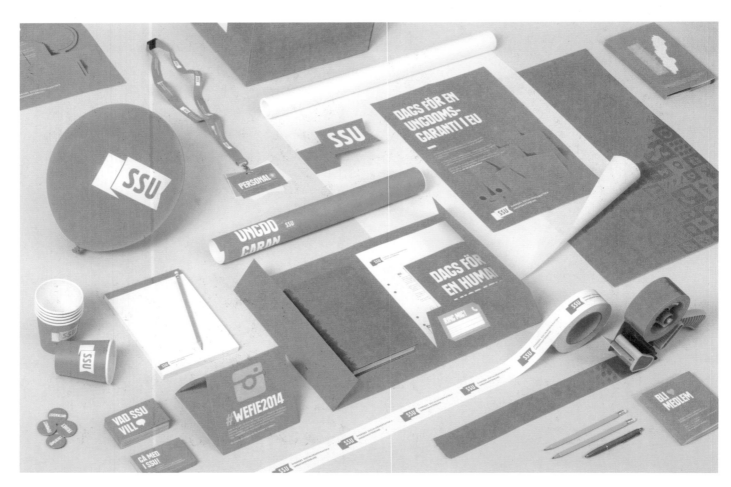

Design: SNASK

CMYK

Arrels Identity

Arrels, which means "roots" in English, is a Barcelona based footwear brand that makes shoes for the urban market. Creating the identity meant finding the right balance between their urban look and their rural roots and between being handmade and mass-produced. This duality is reflected in the two colors of the identity and in the pattern created for the boxes and the shoes. The idea was also carried over to the brochure. The design of the pattern plays with the idea that if you were to rip up all the layers of concrete which cover the urban landscape underneath, you would find the original, natural surface of the earth.

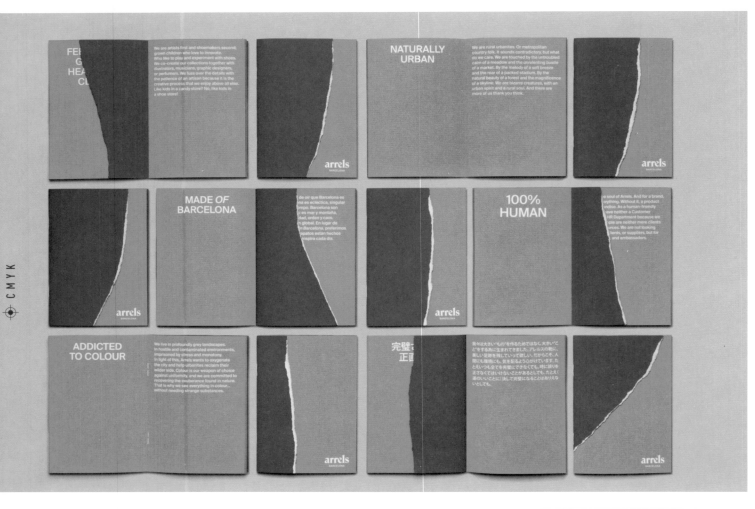

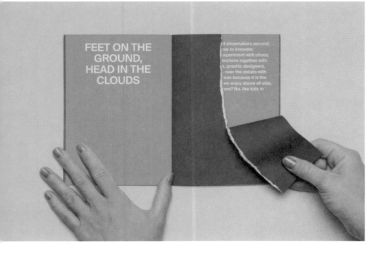

Design: Hey Studio

Apex Branding

Apex Studio is a new graphic design studio with the initial task of creating its own identity. The concept was to develop a brand that could be promoted as a "visual graphic blog," where inspirations and a methodical process could be reflected in the main logo, presenting itself not as a static image, but rather as an ever-changing form that does not lose its true identity. Colors are limited in the whole design, but they lighten it up.

Design: Apex Studio

Media Tube

Visual identity for Media Tube.
Media Tube is an independent art gallery that exhibits and presents contemporary media artists within a progressive curatorial framework.
It also publishes a booklet which shares art news and criticism of international movies and media art pieces. NA played with the idea of the radio spectrum and used a tailor-made typeface for Media Tube's identity.

Design: Not Available (NA)

The Chocolate Fish Rebranding

Rebranding concept for The Chocolate Fish.
The Chocolate Fish is a New Zealand chocolate brand, which sells chocolate sardines
to children. The aim is to make an attractive visual identity with a handcrafted touch.
The simple two colors of white and blue generate some elegance.

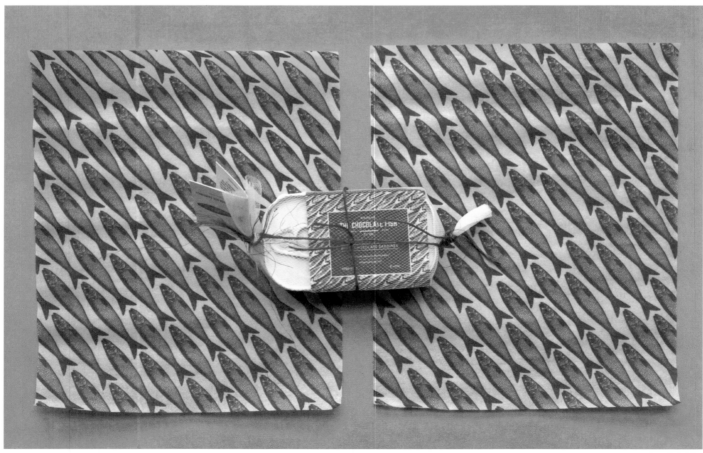

Design: Laura Beretti

Intersect Origins | Nº 001/2

Intersect Origins is a book about Chinese history. It provides a special perspective for reader to look again at the representative ancient objects in Chinese culture. The book was not designed in the same way of its types. It uses bright colors to make for a modern aesthetic for the objects.

CMYK

Design: Ori Studio / Maxim Cormier & Xuechen Fan

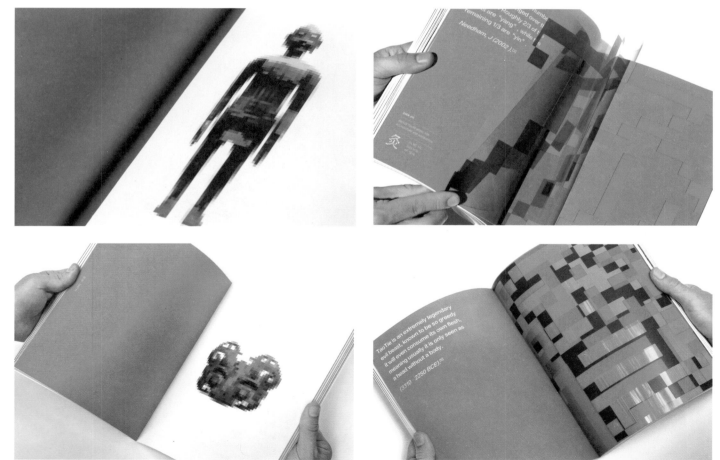

Mod Culture Publication

Mod is a British youth subculture of the early to mid-1960s, focused on fashion, scooter culture and modern jazz. *Mod Culture* looks back to the culture and art of the period. Only two colors are used to create maximum contrast and stability, as well as to emphasize the beauty of typographic elements. Words are broken down into individual letters or syllables, arranged randomly to create visual impact.

Design: Holly Le

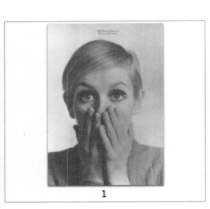

1

2

3

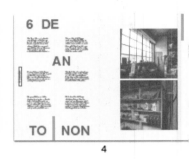

4

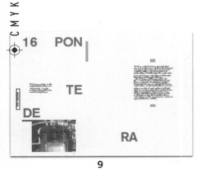

9

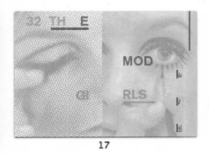

10

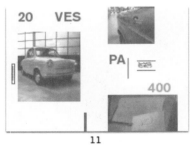

11

12

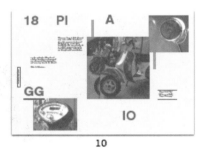

17

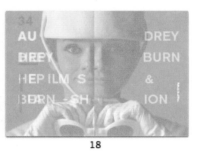

18

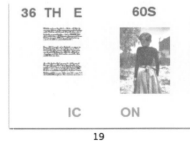

19

2Q

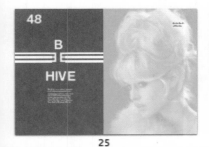

25

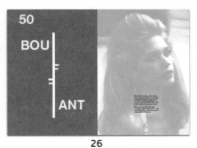

26

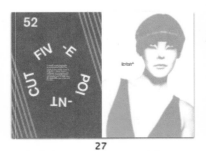

27

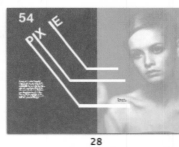

28

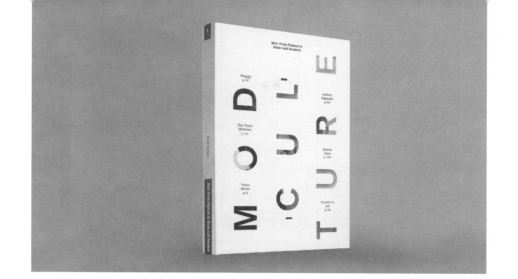

8
THE
UN TOLD
STO RY

5

10
V S

6

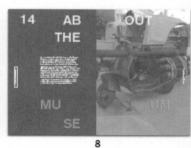

12
FR OM
THE
MU S
.19 46 51 72 79 .2013

7

14 AB OUT
THE
MU SE UM

8

MODS

13

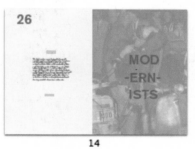

26
MOD -ERN- ISTS

14

28
MODS
ROCKERS

15

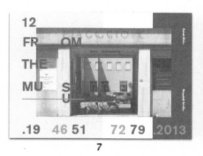

30
SCOO -TER- ISTS

16

40
THE RO MAN HO LI

21

42
HOW TO
STE AL
A MILL ION

22

44
FUN NY
FA CE

23

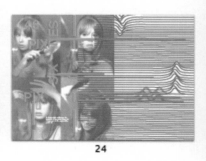

24

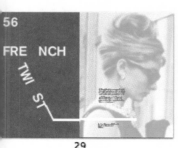

56
FRE NCH
TWI ST

29

58
FL IP
OU T

30

60
TWI GGY
THE MINI MINI THE
GI RL WO RLD*

31

62

32

To the Future Me

An album cover designed for Chinese singer Li Qi's very first solo album, To the Future Me.
The album was designed like an envelope full of memories, which contains postcards, letterhead, CD and poster. Every song is illustrated on an individual postcard and the lyric is placed on the reverse side of the postcard, which works like the postcards are kept for years in the envelope for memory. Additionally, it comes with an empty letterhead for people to write a message for their future self. A light color palette is used to work with the memory atmosphere.

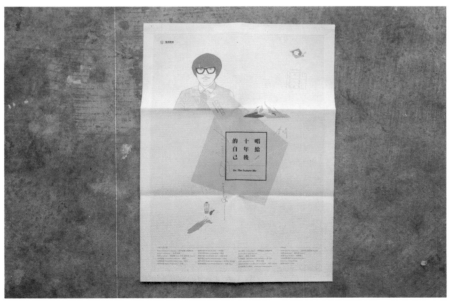

Design: Magdalene Wong

Film Directors Dictionary

This project includes brochures distributed to the audience at a cinema to provide information about movie directors and their styles. Each director has his own unique font and color. But the colors are all from the same color family and work well when placed together. There are 9 folding posters, each one has an A3 size and folds 8 times.

◈ C M Y K

Design: Or Shaaltiel

CMYK Color Swatch Calendar 2016

The Color Swatch Calendar combines a daily calendar with a professional color swatch book. Each day a color stripe can be torn off and new color combinations appear. Printed on coated and uncoated paper, the stripes can be collected to create color matching fans with the use of bookbinder screws, and the exact CMYK data are printed on every stripe. The international edition of the Color Swatch Calendar comes with 371 carefully selected CMYK colors plus a box to collect all those lovely colors.

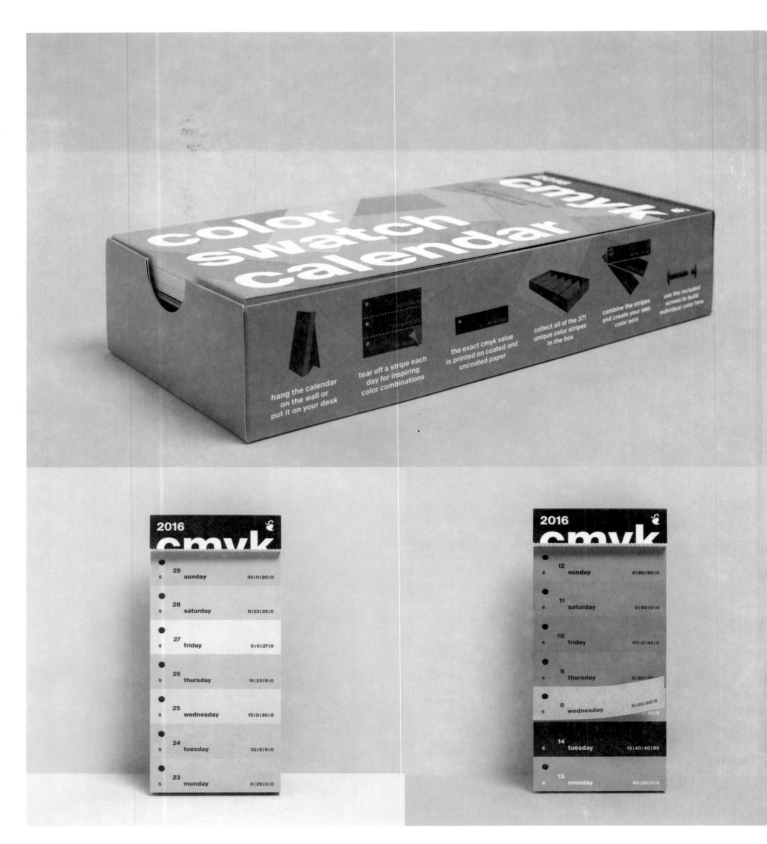

Design: Peter von Freyhold

Eternal April

This brochure is designed for a Polish theatre in Poznań. The red color is crucial to make this unique design. The red edges echo the same colored elements in the brochure body, as well as create a strong contrast with the black cover.

Design: Marcin Markowski / Yo Studio

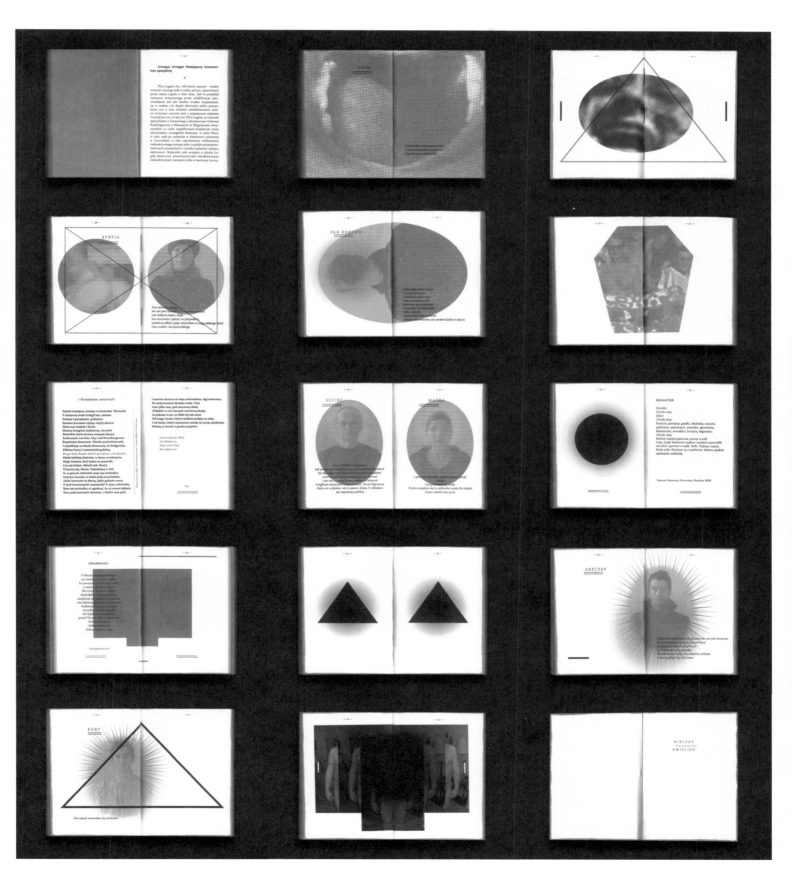

Stamp Design for Hungarian Folk Tales

Bigibogi included some extra fun in this stamp design. There are some stamps either in the form of sheetlet or block that is part of a "puzzle." So by collecting all the individual pieces, you can see the full picture. The pastel tone and illustrated style work perfectly with a folk tale theme.

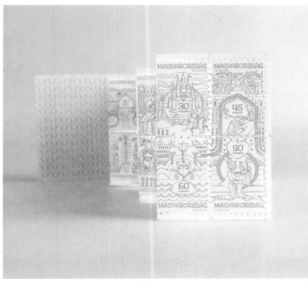 

Design: Boglárka Nádi / bigibogi

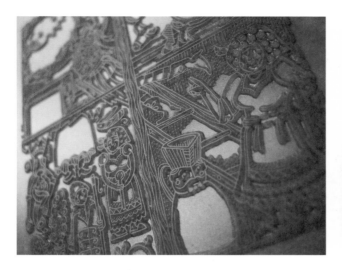

NOMADS Identity 2013

Identity for an advertising agency NOMADS.
The design was based on the idea of "tribal markings." Colored symbols are used to represent data about the "tribe" members. Each employee gets two sets of business cards: a formal one with their own portrait and a second set with a "tribal" pattern relating to their own personal "meta data." The patterns on the business cards create a huge "tribal" pattern when properly ordered.

CMYK

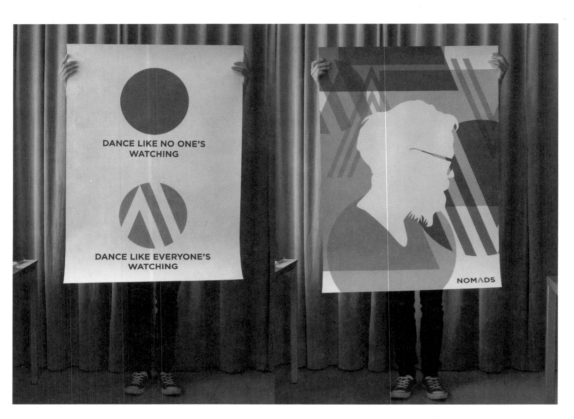

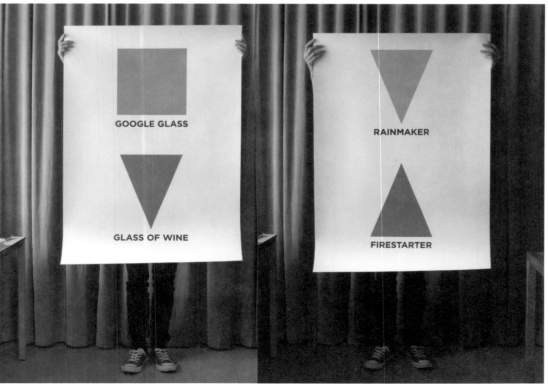

Design: me studio / Martin Pyper

C. Cosmetics and Care

Brand identity for C. Cosmetics and Care, an all-natural-ingredient beauty shop located in Amsterdam.
To fit with C. Cosmetics' philosophy of living a healthy life, the business cards were made from actual edible paper as well as seed paper that will spout wildflowers when planted. The bright blossoms stand out on the cards and packaging while they give a hint as to what you might find when you open the package.

Design: byRosa

Idealism and Functionalism

This book talks about idealism and functionalism, two theories which had great impact on design in the last century. The designer used different colored shapes and a grid structure to demonstrate the two theories visually. The red circle represents metaphysics while the black part symbolizes functionalism. And the purple element signifies the interplay of the two theories and their effect on our society.

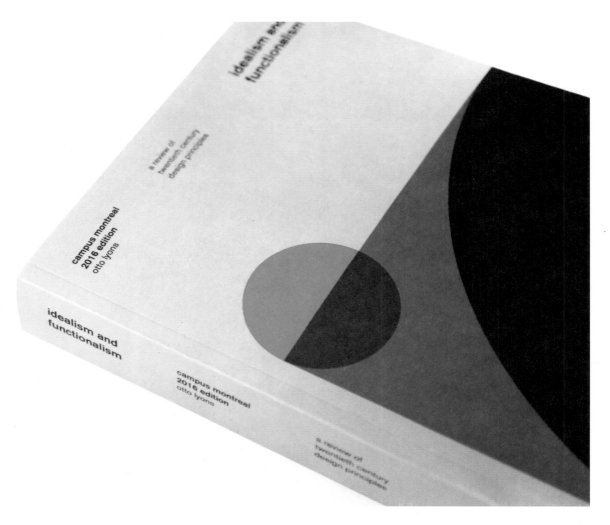

Design: Ori Studio / Maxim Cormier & Xuechen Fan

Menus for New Year Party

Bica do Sapato is a Portugal restaurant and celebrates every New Year with a party. These menus were designed for the parties from 2007-2011. The menus' rich colors create the atmosphere of a New Year.

Design: Diogo Potes

WHAT

IS

PMS

Like CMYK colors, the Pantone Matching System (PMS), is a color reproduction system in the printing industry. A PMS color is always referred to as a spot color or a solid color, which is any color generated by a pure or mixed ink that is printed using a single run. PMS colors are preferred by graphic designers owing to four properties. First, the PMS colors are beyond the printed CMYK gamut, which means they can reproduce more colors than CMYK inks.

Second, the hue of each PMS color is unique and can be found in the Pantone Matching System, which guarantees accurate color conversion.

PANTONE® Basic Colors

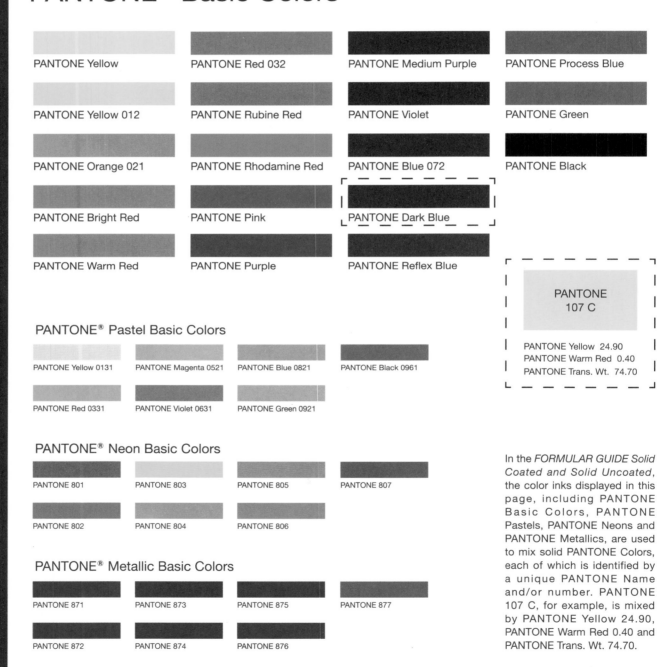

PANTONE Yellow	PANTONE Red 032	PANTONE Medium Purple	PANTONE Process Blue
PANTONE Yellow 012	PANTONE Rubine Red	PANTONE Violet	PANTONE Green
PANTONE Orange 021	PANTONE Rhodamine Red	PANTONE Blue 072	PANTONE Black
PANTONE Bright Red	PANTONE Pink	PANTONE Dark Blue	
PANTONE Warm Red	PANTONE Purple	PANTONE Reflex Blue	

PANTONE® Pastel Basic Colors

PANTONE Yellow 0131	PANTONE Magenta 0521	PANTONE Blue 0821	PANTONE Black 0961
PANTONE Red 0331	PANTONE Violet 0631	PANTONE Green 0921	

PANTONE
107 C

PANTONE Yellow 24.90
PANTONE Warm Red 0.40
PANTONE Trans. Wt. 74.70

PANTONE® Neon Basic Colors

PANTONE 801	PANTONE 803	PANTONE 805	PANTONE 807
PANTONE 802	PANTONE 804	PANTONE 806	

PANTONE® Metallic Basic Colors

PANTONE 871	PANTONE 873	PANTONE 875	PANTONE 877
PANTONE 872	PANTONE 874	PANTONE 876	

In the *FORMULAR GUIDE Solid Coated and Solid Uncoated*, the color inks displayed in this page, including PANTONE Basic Colors, PANTONE Pastels, PANTONE Neons and PANTONE Metallics, are used to mix solid PANTONE Colors, each of which is identified by a unique PANTONE Name and/or number. PANTONE 107 C, for example, is mixed by PANTONE Yellow 24.90, PANTONE Warm Red 0.40 and PANTONE Trans. Wt. 74.70.

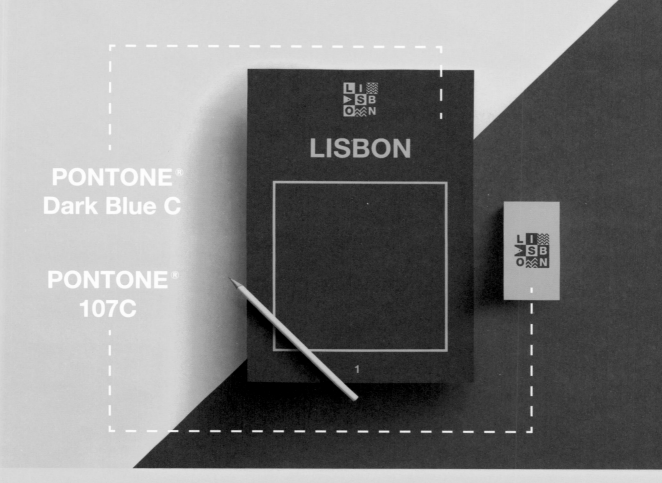

PONTONE® Dark Blue C

PONTONE® 107C

Third, a PMS ink is always printed at 100% and has no dot pattern. But PMS inks can also be printed in "screens" or "halftones" to simulate various shades of a color as four-color printing does.

Fourth, produced based on the subtractive color model, PMS inks feature low value but high saturation.

When you print any PMS colors, a standardized color chart is needed as the colors on computer don't look exactly the same as the printed ones. But we can preview the printing color effect and use the accurate color by referring to the color chart. The most popular color chart today is from Pantone LLC.

Pantone LLC is the world-renowned authority on color and provides color systems for accurate color communication across a variety of industries, primarily printing, and also in the manufacture of fabric and plastics, etc. The PANTONE® system is known worldwide as the standard language for color communication from designer to manufacturer to retailer to customer. Pantone provides various color charts for many industries such as print, fashion and home, and plastics. Each Pantone color has a unique color name, which allows us to specify a color easily. In the Pantone color chart for the printing industry, for example, every color name is made up of three or four numbers following by the letter "C" or "U," such as Pantone 100 C, Pantone 100 U, Pantone 1205 C, and Pantone 1205 U. "C" means the color is printed on a glossy, coated media while "U" indicates the color is printed on uncoated stock.

PANTONE®

Pantone uses colors to understand and express the emotional texture of people, products and even times. Their beliefs on color helped to establish it as something alive, expressive, and timeless. When we sit down with Laurie Pressman, we certainly feel their passion in colors.

How does Pantone perceive colors? What is it about color that fascinates Pantone so much?

At Pantone we look at color as expression. Color has the unique ability to attract and engage the eye, elicit emotion, enhance any product or environment and ultimately create magic and mood. As Leatrice Eiseman, Executive Director of the Pantone Color Institute, shares in "Colors For Your Every Mood," the right colors and color combinations will stimulate or relax your senses, release happy memories and influence how you relate to others in your environment.

How is Pantone fitting into Asia-Pacific market?

Whether as a source of inspiration or as a way to communicate color choices and control consistency of color across every imaginable surface, texture, material and finish, the Pantone color language standard is used in all industries globally where color plays a critical role. When we consider the Asia-pacific market on its own, we understand that while color family preferences have become more global with the advent of the web and social media, there are specific color shades in these color families which may be more popular in the Asian region. To better support these regional preferences we are looking to create products and material formats that are tailored toward our Asia-pacific based clients.

Laurie Pressman, Vice-President of Pantone Color Institute at Pantone LLC

Annually, Pantone declares a particular color "color of the year"—what are the standards for making the selection of this color? And who is the target group for this standard?

To decide which color to select for our "color of the year," we talk with a broad cross section of designers from around the world who are involved in many different design industries including fashion, home interiors, beauty, industrial and print to find out the colors they think will be important in their businesses for the upcoming year. By talking to designers in a wide-cross section of industries, we can be sure that we forecast a color which will have broad appeal for all age ranges and design markets. We sift through this information to find the color family that is fresh and new, as well as common to many different industries and then narrow it down to a specific shade within that color family that is consumer-friendly and can be used to sell all types of products and packages. In the end, we want people to stop and notice this new color. Seeing a dress, or a tie or even a set of dishes in a new and different color gets the consumers' attention when they are shopping and may just be what's needed to entice them to buy something new.

BELIEF
IN
COLORS

As human evolved with the greatest power of all in nature, we started with finding basic paints to apply on anything and everything, and then our curiosity and the development of industries together propelled us to learn more about the continuous spectrum of colors. With the developing science of color, people utilized professional techniques to exploit more advanced color materials. Since people's vision of color are different, it is difficult to define what a real color is, which brings about color errors in different industries. Therefore, it is necessary to formulate a color standard to specify the use of colors. Pantone and the Natural Color System(NCS) are the standard makers of colors.

In 1960s, Lawrence Herbert was a printer. When a client insisted that the colors printed out were not what he really wanted, Lawrence realized the need for developing an accurate matching system of colors for printers, a formula which could be applied repeatedly. Consequently, Pantone came into being. Pantone has been extracting colors from visual culture as it develops its color system. With different cultural, political or historical backgrounds, there are different representative colors for different times. As a result, Pantone provides color systems and leading technology for the selection and accurate communication of colors across different industries including digital technology, graphic arts, fashion, furnishing, plastics, architecture, interior and paints.

The 20th century is a vital period for color. Due to the revolutionary changes in visual aesthetics, the old standards were replaced by the completely new ones. Influenced by the new technologies, inventions, political environments and the pursuit of individuality, a timeline of colors from Pantone was developed to represent the cultural history of the 20th century.

In the 20th century, the appearance and popularity of the big screen was a striking feature. 1940s was the time for "film noir", which focused on exploring the dark side of society in iconic films such as The Killers, Mildred Pierce, and Shadow of A Doubt, applying black, white and red to express specific characters: for example, Raven and High Risk Red were the representative colors for evil women. At the same time, these colors or films were the reflection of politic bias, the indifference between people and the unsettled conditions of family at that time. When Eastman Kodak broke through technological limitations and launched 35mm color film in the 1950s, the visual effect on the screen became softer and more colorful. Screen goddesses Audrey Hepburn and Grace Kelly led the trend of delicate colors such as pink and light blue.

For clothing, as the Second World War broke out in 1939, all kinds of clothes started to emphasize functionality, which was reflected in the recruiting posters designed by Robert Muchley or newspaper cover design "Willie Gillis at the USO." Tan, Olive Gray, Major Brown, and Paprika were the popular colors at that time. However, when the war ended, people wanted a relaxed and easy environment, so a leisure style of clothes with colors such as Fir, Air Blue, Purple Impression or Maize became popular.

Pantone emerged from printing industry with a strong understanding of visual culture, developing various color systems for different industries for a more intuitive selection of colors, an expanded palette of spot colors, new premium metallics and neons, and Pantone color manager software.

For the fashion, home furnishings and interior design industries, the Pantone Fashion + Home Color System is the primary instrument for designers to select and specify the colors of textile and clothing manufacturing. This system includes 2,100 colors in cotton and paper to assemble new palettes and conceptual color schemes. Pantone also declares a particular color "color of the year" annually, like Turquoise in 2010, Honeysuckle in 2011 and Tangerine Tango in 2012, influencing the trends of product development in areas such as fashion, home furnishings and industrial design.

With Pantone stressing the historical meanings or representations of colors, its color systems are based on research of the typical icons of different times. However, the main goal for the Natural Color System® (NCS) is to establish efficient communication with color for people with different languages or from different industries.

The NCS is published by the Scandinavian Color Institute (Skandinaviska Färginstitutet AB) of Stockholm, Sweden for color communication in architecture, design, manufacturing, research and education. It includes millions of colors which can be perceived by human eyes. Based on the six primary colors, it is established by studying the potential and limitations of human vision. NCS helps customers define and manage color more easily, accurately and consistently by providing NCS-based solutions. The mission of NCS is not only to bring color visions into reality simply and efficiently, but also to communicate with clients easily, even if they speak different languages.

The NCS system is based on the six primary colors perceived by human vision, which are white, black, red, yellow, green and blue. These six primary colors are frequently used in educational toys for children or designs that are appealing for their simplicity. Colors in the NCS are defined by three values, specifying the amount of blackness (darkness), chromaticity (saturation), and a percentage value between two of the colors among red, yellow, green or blue (hue). The complete NCS color notation can also be tagged with a letter giving the version of the NCS color standard that was used to specify the color.

Color is an essential element in architecture design or selecting materials. For architects, there is a common language from NCS, taking the guesswork out of the color discussion. Therefore, NCS creates a platform for efficient communication between architects and suppliers around the world.

In design, the most important thing is to obtain a suitable color. A variety of tools are provided by NCS to simplify and improve the process of selecting the right colors or color combinations for designers, which not only assists them in knowing more about the color trends through various solutions, but also allows them to communicate and specify the colors that are applied in designs accurately to monitor the outcome. The creative process is a difficult one, with countless considerations and variables. Design today needs to be able to control as many of these variables as possible.

For paint and product manufacturers, NCS is a crucial business development tool to increase sales performance in a cost-efficient way. NCS can help improve profitability and efficiency at each step of the color communication process with a number of tools and services, from color collection development to production, marketing and sales. The client's organization also gains a common language that improves efficiency and communications everywhere. For example, for professional painters, NCS is a language that helps them communicate with their clients on the decision of the right colors or color combinations. The key to a successful delivery of a project is clear and understandable communication.

For teachers and corporations, NCS offers the necessary study or educational material needed to teach The Universal Language of Color, aiding students or companies in grasping a language that is an international standard. The knowledge which NCS gives can be applied across any given industry regardless of language, materials or market sectors. The NCS also developed educational material for institutions where students will, ultimately, work professionally with color challenges regarding design, specification, production or evaluation. The material offers a unique opportunity to work with precise color samples. The study material trains the eye to recognize similarities and differences among colors. This develops the skills needed to systematically arrange, describe and communicate the properties of colors.

Laurie Pressman

Projects

La Fábrica del Taco

These designs were made by BOSQUE, a design studio in Argentina, for the restaurant La Fábrica del Taco. The bold and colorful designs are shown on menus, sauces, uniforms, murals, posters and furniture, which creates a warm space.

Design: BOSQUE

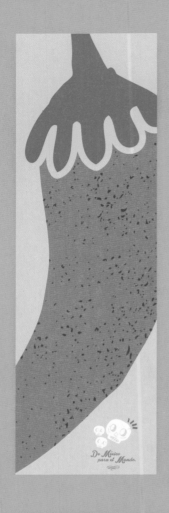

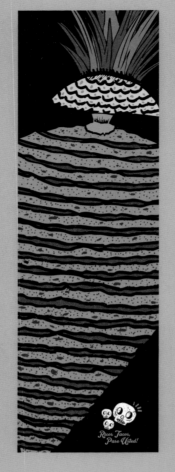

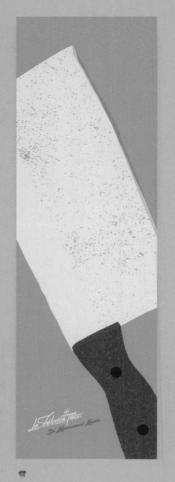

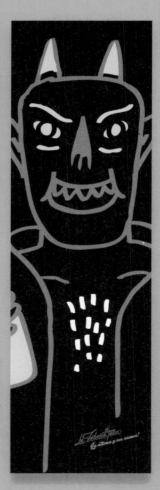

LA ULTI MA y N OS VA MOS.

La Fabrica Taco

GORRITI 5062
BUENOS AIRES

CHICHIS PA'LA BANDA!

GORRITI 5062
BUENOS AIRES

GORRITI 5062
BUENOS AIRES

El Postre

El Postre is a pastry boutique in Mexico. The boutique wishes to adapt itself to the present market, so the designers gave the brand a lift to achieve a modern look and feel. They selected a range of red and pink tones to form the color palette as well as the gold foil which is used as an elegant accent. To complete the system, a multiple array of patterns were developed and implemented on each packaging, achieving a unique and authentic experience similar to receiving a special gift.

Design: Anagrama

Kollage Magazine

This print for Kollage Magazine, which is completely Risograph printed, is inspired by ancient Persian miniatures and rugs combined with modern techniques and influences. This creates a psychedelic world which is an ongoing theme in Nick Liefhebber's work. The special inks like gold and deep blue enhance a mysterious impression.

Design: Liefhebber Design

OIMU Octagonal Matchbox

This project was intended to support the declining match industry by means of package redesign. The octagonal box and the gradients contribute to the artistic matchbox.

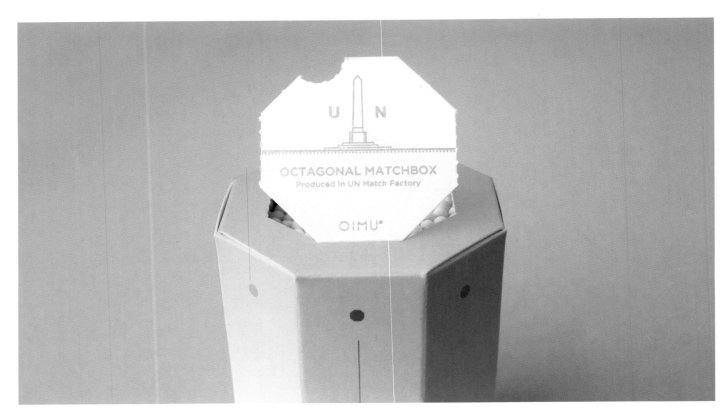

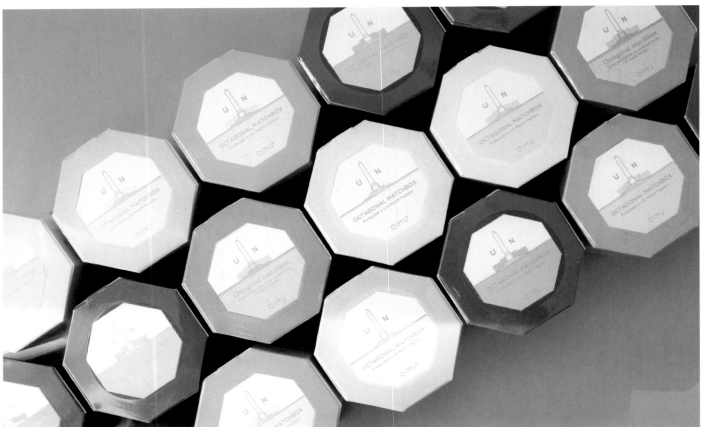

Design: OIMU

P M S

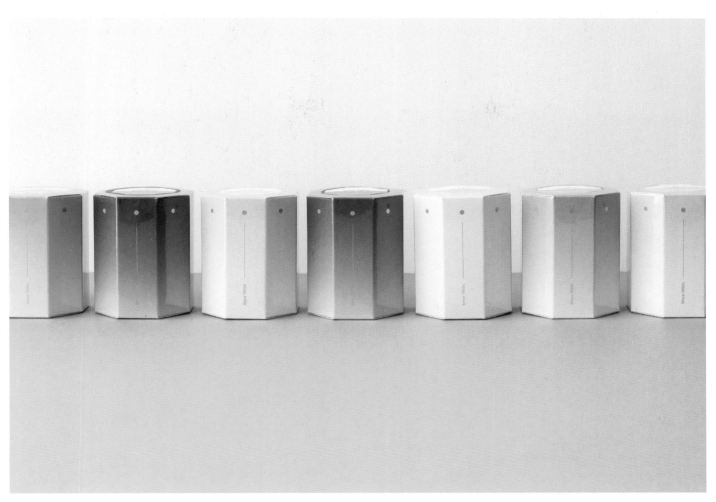

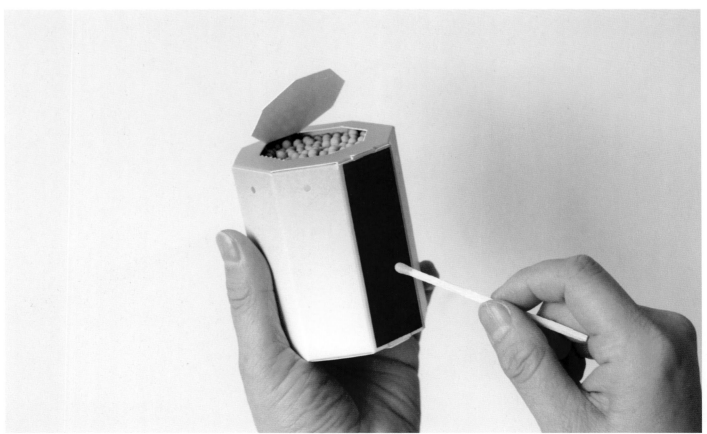

ENTREMÉS

Entremés is a culinary factory catering for social gatherings. The products it provides are all linked together by the use of one ingredient: parsley. Thus, the company incorporates the parsley in its logo, accentuating it as a brand key ingredient and the natural color of parsley is also adopted for the visual identity to create a refreshing quality.

Waldo Trommler Paints

Waldo Trommler Paints (WTP) is a small Finnish company planning to enter the US market and desires to stand out among its competitors. Reynolds and Reyner designed a brand with no corporate colors. WTP simply features common design elements that are recolored in a wide array of bright hues, depending on the application. This helps WTP not only achieve its goal of standing out, but helps cast itself as the friendliest paint company on shelves today.

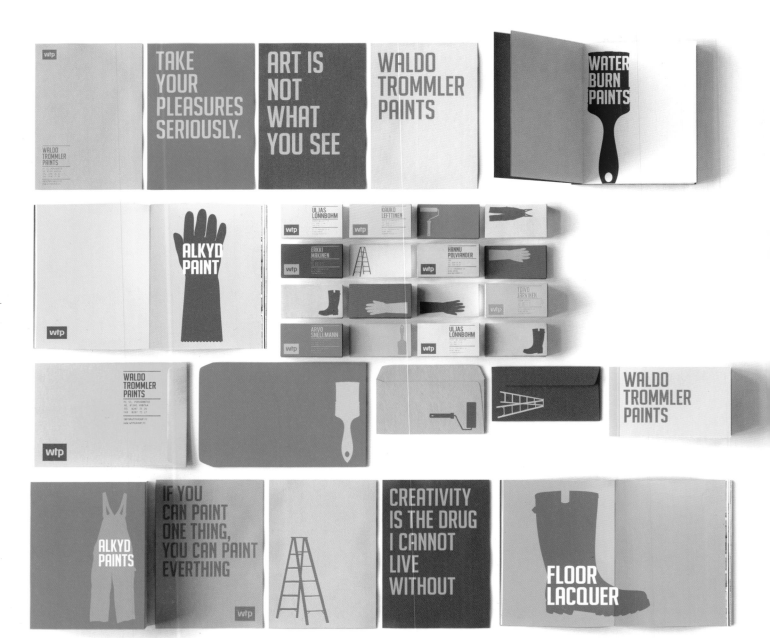

Design: Reynolds and Reyner

THIS World Music Fest@ Formosa

This visual identity for THIS World Music Fest@ Formosa, a music festival took place in Taiwan uses two bold colors, namely red and blue, to create a striking contrast and a lively picture, which reflects the free spirit of the festival. The white part balances the two bright colors well.

Design: Onion Design Associates

3D Tetrahedron Business Cards

The business card was designed for a product designer to use in her degree show. In order to showcase her work in making forms and shapes, Sumaya Mahadevan developed a tetrahedron card in aquamarine. There were folded examples on display to invite visitors to make their own tetrahedrons.

PANTONE
P 124–11 C

PANTONE
P 124–13 C

Design: Sumaya Mahadevan

ReARTlity Show

ReARTlity Show is a non-traditional exhibition which shows the audience the process of making arts instead of display finished artworks. The designers used bright color palette and hilarious illustration to echo this unusual way. The color contrast adds vigor to the brochure.

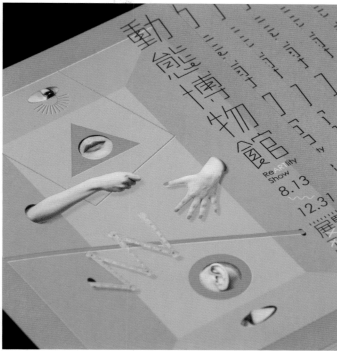

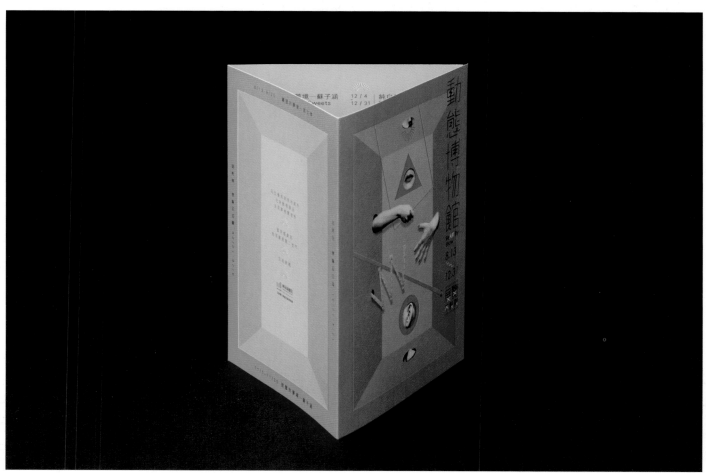

Design: Houth

Katowice Street Art Festival 2015

The identity of Katowice Street Art Festival 2015 impresses audience with its rich colors. The contrasting colors are applied to the poster to create a strong visual effect. Each poster keeps a no-more-than-three-color color palette, which helps the creation of a rich but clean picture.

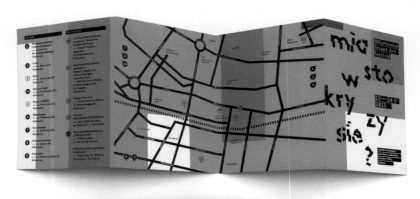

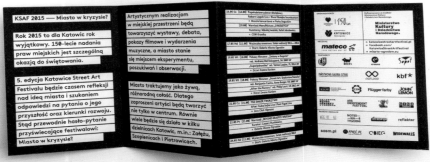

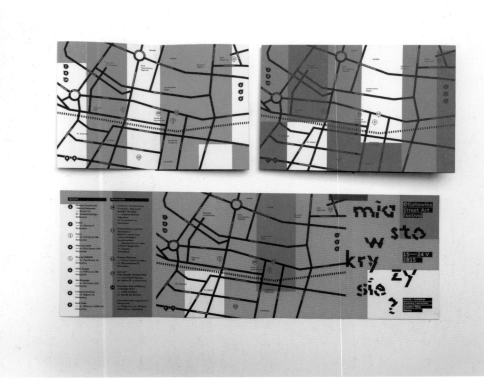

Design: Marta Gawin

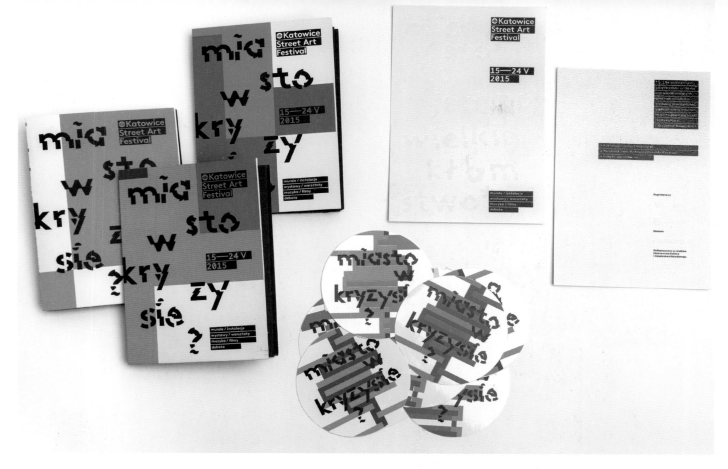

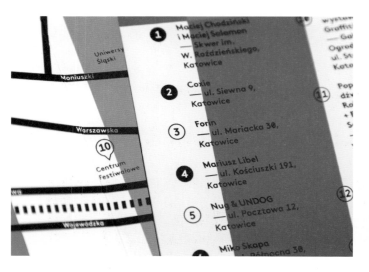

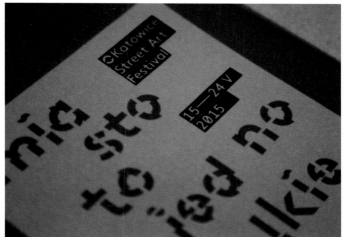

Latin American Design Festival

Graphic identity for Latin American Design Festival (LAD).
LAD is an organization aiming to promote Latin American design globally. Its identity impressed people by the multicolor elements, from the textiles and woven fabric from the Andes to the colorful and geometric shapes largely used in the Andean Community to the tropical identity of the rainforest tribes and cumbia and chichi posters. Neon colors are used widely all over Latin America, especially in Perú, where the first edition of the festival took place. All the banners and signage of the festival are made in a traditional way which combines silkscreen and hand-painted fabric with neon colors.

Design: IS Creative Studio

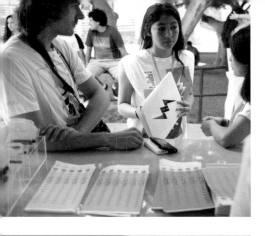

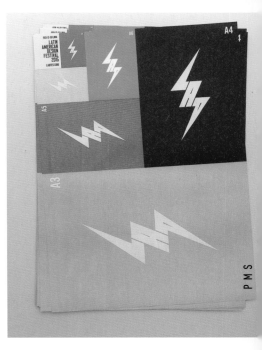

DELIZET

Packaging design for D E L I Z E T & c o, a chocolate brand.
D E L I Z E T keeps its products limited and exclusive. The vivid color palette for its packaging
makes it eye-catching and unique, suggesting D E L I Z E T's essence.

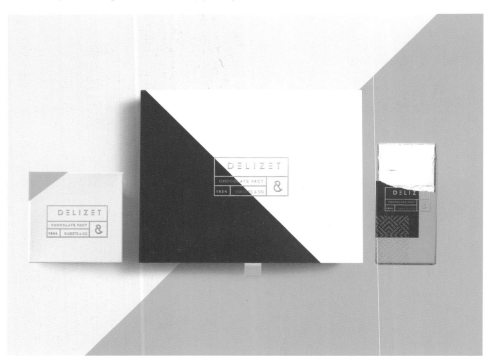

◈ P M S

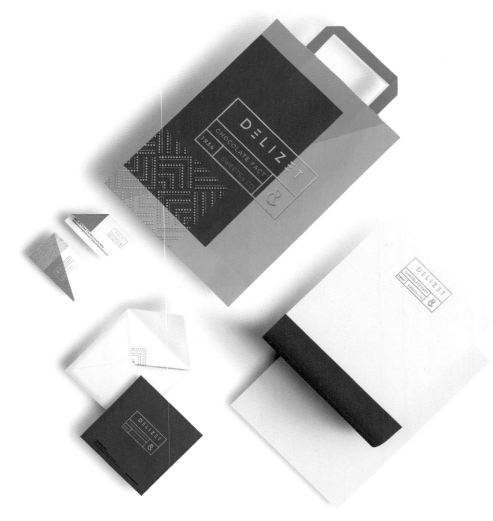

Design: Marina Porte

Sebazzo Visual Identity

This series of business card finds its axis in the letter "A," the center element of the logotype. With dual pastel palettes for each model, they combine for mesmerizing images when placed side by side.

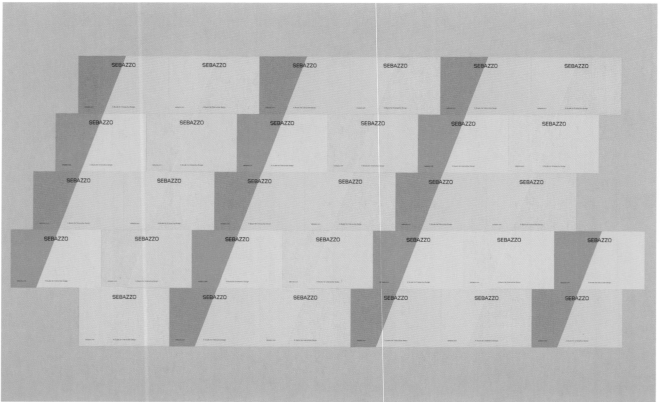

Design: Bunch

Jameson Limited Edition Bottle

Jameson is an Irish liquor brand. This is Jameson's fifth annual limited-edition bottle. The overall design is a way of paying homage to Dublin. It is an artwork featuring a map of roads with images of Dublin landmarks. The prominent green color keeps the design consistent with the bottle. With a metallic color and clever typography, the slogan "Wherever I roam, it's Dublin my heart calls home" is highlighted.

Design: Steve Simpson

Theatre Runway

This interesting poster takes elements from several dramas such as *Tanz der sieben Schleier* and *La Traviata*.
Important parts were emphasized by the bold colors.

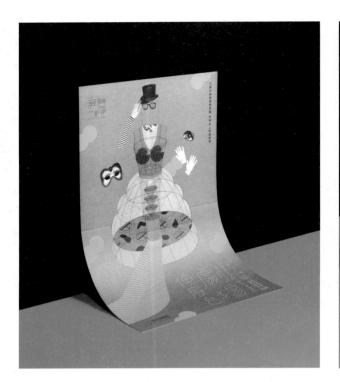

Design: Houth

Oveja Negra Lowe

The logo and identity design expresses the merging of two companies, one of which is international and the other local. An acronym of the two companies' names is created to communicate the idea of two becoming one, allowing the number 1 to double as a lower-case "l." The witty character of the local company is represented by a "black sheep." It plays a starring role in the identity, changing locations and colors randomly to continually surprise and engage.

Design: Blok Design

David & Estibaliz Wedding Invitation

The invitation was covered with a neon yellow color, which adds fresh and bright elements to the wedding. The name of each guest is handwritten with black over irregular neon yellow spray lines. The gold engraving is for the date and the wedding protagonists.

P M S

Design: Mubien

The Pictograms

The Pictograms is a book about the application of Hanzi in the modern design world. The cover uses two colors, black and fluorescent green. The solid black background makes allusion to the long history of Hanzi while the neon green symbolizes its use in design under a modern context. Meanwhile, the sharp contrast they yield is impressive.

Design: SendPoints Publishing

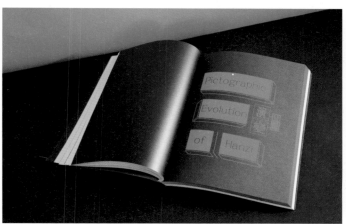

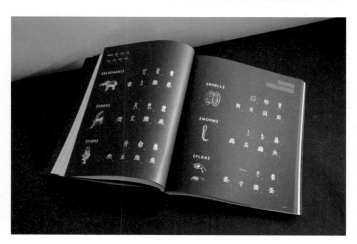

Chick Chirik Wishlist Service

Chick Chirik provides considerate gift packaging services by varying color schemes.
Gold glitter is for the general gifts. Children's gifts are wrapped with colorful illustrations. And turquoise is used for wedding events.

Design: anabolic

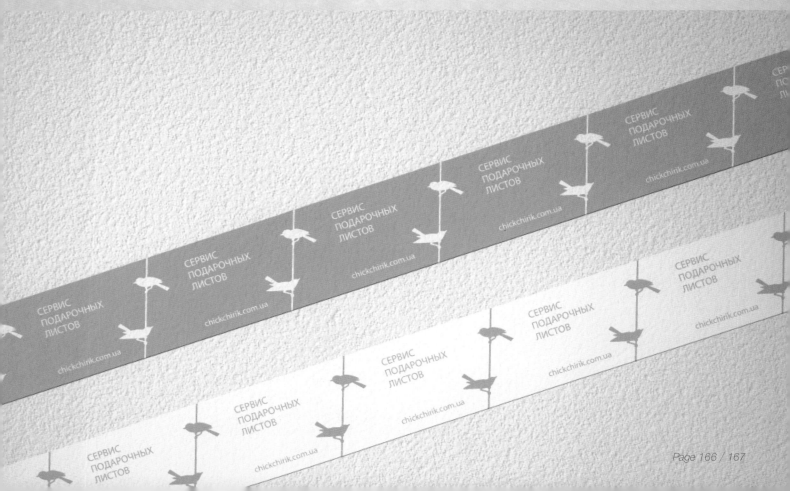

Manipulated Inspiration

This book is a visual journey involving the artists who inspired the designer by helping to shape his creative mind. The book is a tribute to them and their work. To create the book, the designer photocopied pages from other design, art and photography books. He then found pieces of paper left on the floor and printed over these pages. He printed and double-printed onto the different paper stocks to create a unique composition for this book. The book consists of only 34 pages, perfectly bound by hand and inkjet printed on mixed paper stocks. The colored pages were printed with UV reactive luminous acrylic ink, and various colors were used to highlight his favorite pieces of work.

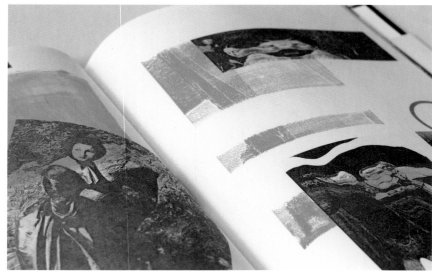

Design: David Newman

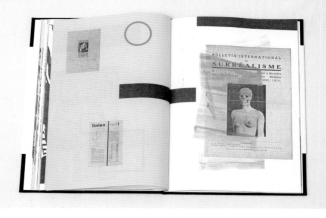

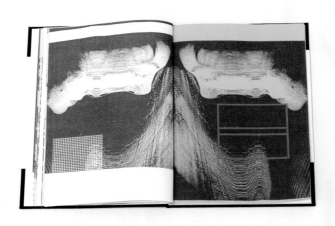

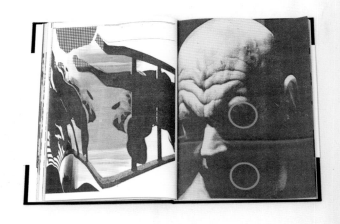

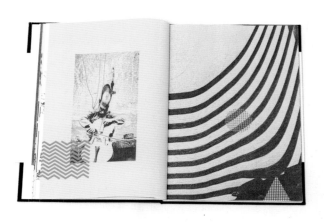

QI Eyewear

Branding identity for QI, a Mexican eyewear company.
When deciding the color palette for this work, the designers used spot colors to achieve a pure extraction of the colors of the "zarape," a Mexican fabric full of tradition and culture. Two Pantone neon colors were picked to create a strong contrast with the pastel tones.

Design: Karla Heredia Martínez

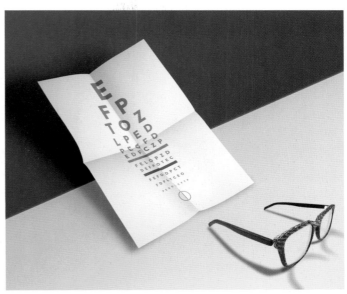

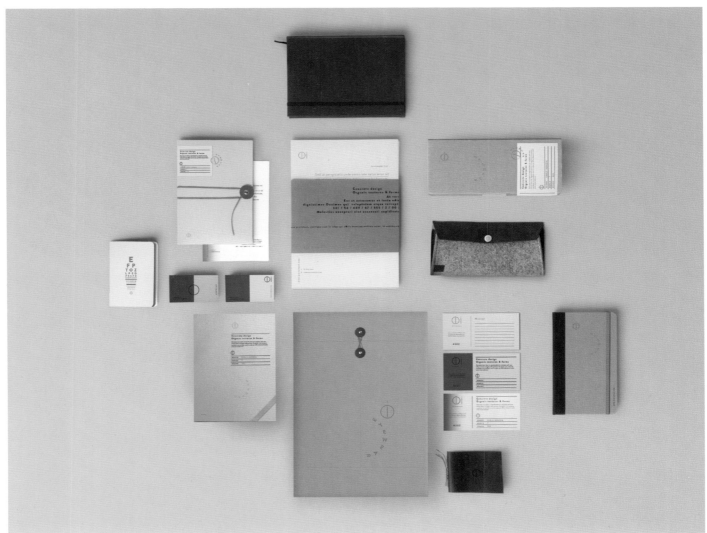

Doméstico

Doméstico cantina's identity, and packaging are simple but elegant. The purple/blue palette contributes greatly to this visual effect.

Design: MANIFIESTO FUTURA, for FUTURA

Teastories

Teastories is a tea store offering a wide variety of selected premium tea products. Anagrama made an allusion to the flavor and aroma of tea in a minimalistic and approachable way, using brush strokes with a subtle color palette throughout the brand's packaging.

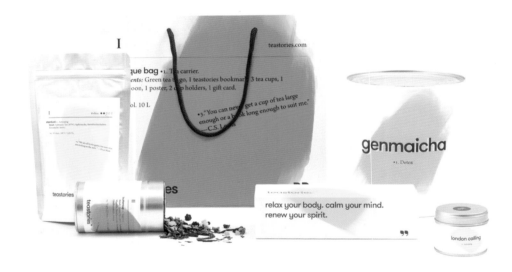

Design: Anagrama

assam (bio)

• 1. Activating

energize your work, life and spirit.
you are amazing and full of energy.

berry crush

• 1. Seductive

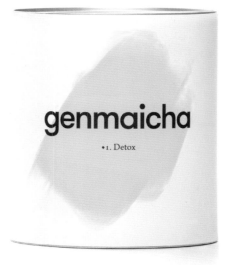

genmaicha

• 1. Detox

Saho.Lab Branding

The design team used a warm color combination for the identity—sunny yellow as the main color and soft pastel colors including green, blue and red, which are associated with new plants, fruits and brooks—to create a warm and gentle impression.

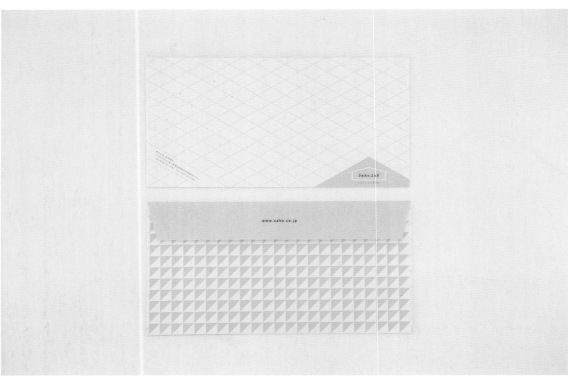

Design: nottuo

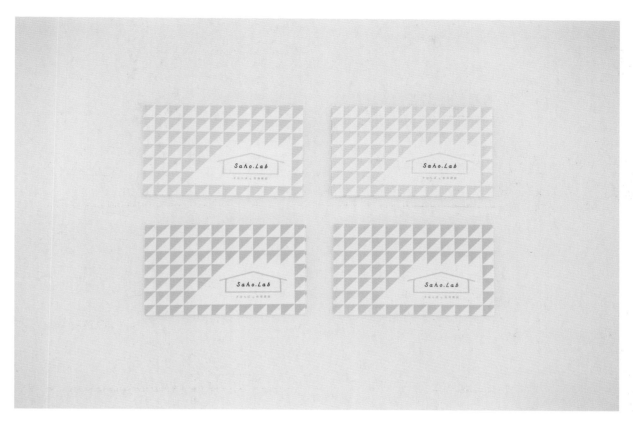

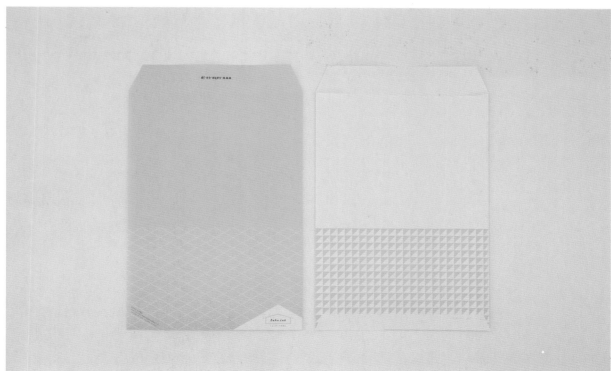

CARTOGRAPHICS: Designing the Modern Map

CARTOGRAPHICS: Designing the Modern Map is a book about modern map design. To correspond to this topic, the book cover was developed based on a map. PANTONE 232 C and PANTONE 285C are adopted for the map to create a strong visual effect. At the same time, the sharp contrast they generate underlines the map's structure, which enhances audience's perception of the book theme. The grey color makes a balance between the two strong colors.

P M S

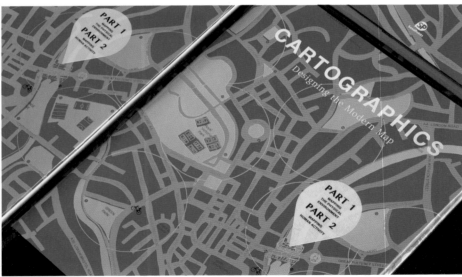

Design: SendPoints Publishing

This is Lisbon

This work was created as a response to Pantone's brief for D&AD New Blood Awards, "reimagine your hometown through color."
Lisbon is all about two colors. The bright blue of the morning sky, of the famous "azulejos" (ceramic tiles, a form of Portuguese art), of the Atlantic meets the sunny yellow in the sun almost constantly illuminating the city, as well as in electric trams criss-crossing the city center through esplanades and tiny streets.

Design: Yana K

Mohé

Mohé is a clothing brand dedicated to women who are not afraid to break rules in their daily outfits and love a little bit of vintage style with bold colors and shapes. Woodie created an elegant and simple identity focusing on typography, basic shapes and distinct colors. Dark grey, which is always stylish and fashionable, adds a chic and smart character to the brand. A combination of different shades of red and pink, often found in women's outfits, provide energy and power to their personalities.

Design: Wojciech Zalot & Gosia Zalot

Wedding Invitation

Unlike traditional weddings, this one was held on a mountain. Bold colors and interesting illustrations were the main elements for the wedding invitation, creating a unique wedding image.

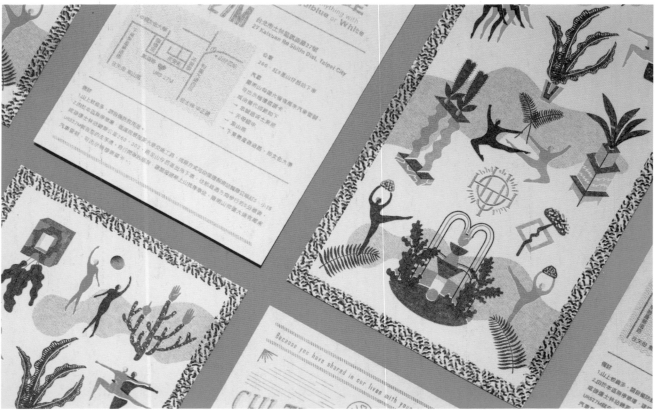

Design: HOUTH

Aloa Input – Mars etc.

Moby Digg designed a new album artwork for Aloa Input's "Mars etc." The designers used two contrast colors, red and blue, to create a sharp visual effect. Blue dots covering the red background are arrayed in a flowing way. The quirky blue typography adds a surreal touch.

P+C MORR MUSIC 2015   LC10387

01 FAR AWAY SUN
02 PERRY
03 VAMPIRE SONG
04 OH BROTHER
05 THE DOOR
06 21ST CENTURY TALE
07 HOLD ON
08 BLABLA THEORY
09 KRK BLUES
10 MAD AS HELL
11 RUTH THE COMMUNIST

MORR MUSIC, PO BOX 550141, 10371 BERLIN, GERMANY
WWW.MORRMUSIC.COM – MORE INFORMATION ON PRESS.MORRMUSIC.COM

Design: Moby Digg

Germán Torres Business Cards

Business cards for the Illustrator German Torres, who draws in La Trastería.

A two-color split fountain was used to recreate the transformation from human to werewolf and black ink for the other details. Letterpress printed on 600gsm cotton paper.

PMS

Design: LA TRASTERÍA

MúzeumCafé Books

MúzeumCafé Books are published by the Museum of Fine Arts in Budapest. The series aims to bring a breath of fresh air to Hungarian book culture. They were printed with the use of FM halftone screening, duplex printing and the application of Pantone Cool Gray 8U and Pantone 805 U direct colors. The bright orange color covering much of the book creates a unified whole.

Design: Lead82

GYÖRGY PÉTER
MÚZEUM. A TANULÓ-HÁZ
MÚZEUMELMÉLETI ESETTANULMÁNYOK
MÚZEUMCAFÉ KÖNYVEK
1. KÖTET

múzeumcafé

Los Bravo Brothers

A book printing for the Bravo Brothers, a circus family.
The book cover and back are silkscreen printed with a florescent orange on black Plike paper. This allows the color to stand out. The use of Rives Tradition paper for the illustrations in the book accents their colors.

Design: José Luís Sousa Dias

Counting the Days

Wedding invitation for a Sicilian bride and a Dutch groom.
The invitation was printed in two colors, red as a symbol of Sicily and orange as the
national color of the Netherlands, on vintage paper by Arjo Wiggins.

Design: Until Sunday

9 Questions

A promotional gift designed for Boutique Creativa to send to its customers.

Boutique Creativa's brand color, Pantone Fluo 811C, worked with three other colors—metallic gold, silver and a plain black—to ensure legibility of the small-sized text for this board game.

Design: Until Sunday

PMS

"Zhuang Sheng Ci" Show

Visual design for a graduation show titled "Zhuang Sheng Ci"（状声词）, meaning "onomatopoeia" in English.
A focus was placed on the color palette. A persistence-of-vision effect was created by the striking contrast of the colors. The metal color is overprinted to visually express the tempo of sound: strong and weak, fast and slow.

Graphic Designer: Chun-Ta Chu / Exhibition Designer: Hsin-Wei Su / Creative Director: Yung-Cheng Chen / Art Director: Ching-Yi Lin

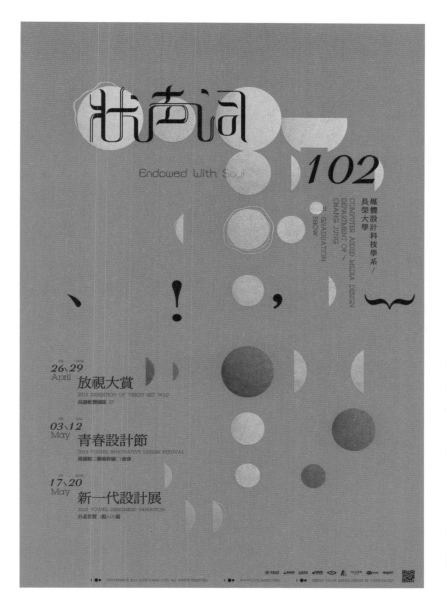

平面設計

朱
俊
達

CHU. CHUN-TA

facebook.com/dada.ju.5
j120015866@hotmail.com
0919317303

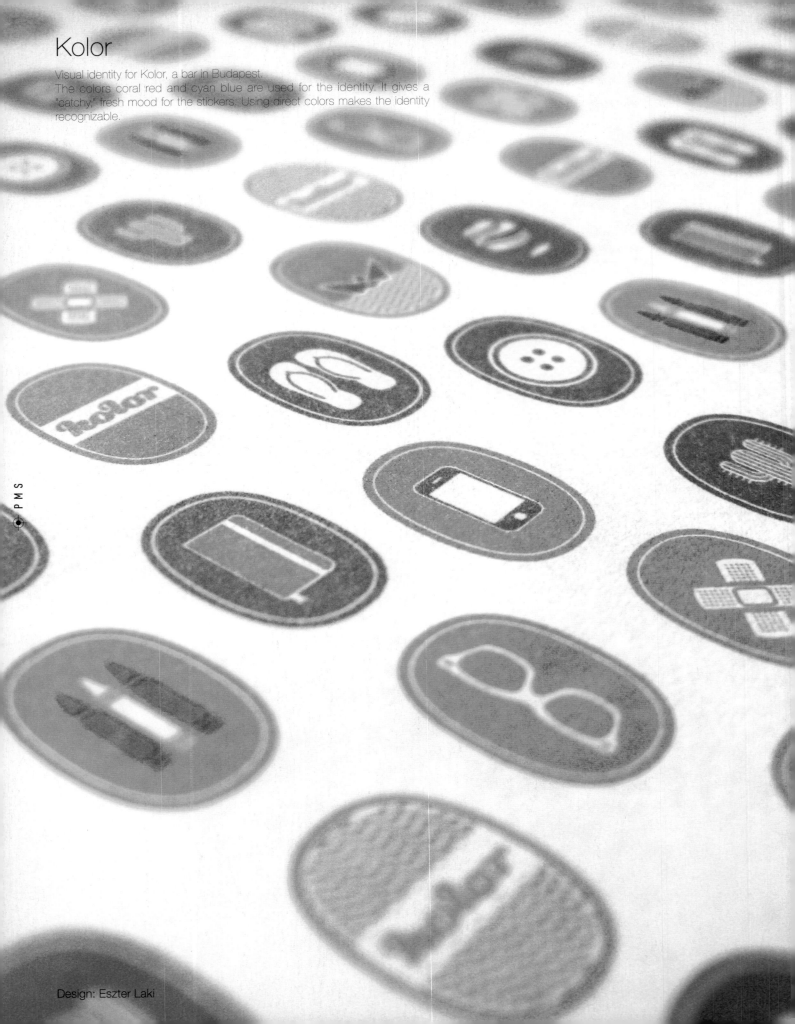

Kolor

Visual identity for Kolor, a bar in Budapest.
The colors coral red and cyan blue are used for the identity. It gives a "catchy," fresh mood for the stickers. Using direct colors makes the identity recognizable.

P M S

Design: Eszter Laki

Try Angle Paper #03

Try Angle Paper #03 is a handmade silkscreen poster presenting the objects in ma studio. The blue and orange contrast makes a vibrant picture. The dot pattern is a bonus to the design.

Design: Triangle-Studio

try
angle
paper
#03

트라이앵글 페이퍼는
트라이앵글-스튜디오의
디자인 간행물로,
만물을 바라보는 구성원들의
다양한 시선을 통해
디자인으로 세상과 소통하는
작은 움직임입니다.

만물과 소통하라.

TRIANGLE-STUDIO
Arts&Graphic Design Partner

서울시 마포구 합정동 356 9 4층(R)
Tel. 02 3144 2674
info@triangle-studio.co.kr
www.triangle-studio.co.kr

lights
효과 도우미

try
angle
paper
#03

in
ma
studio

heater
공장난로

plants
질긴 생역

steel chair
바지 조심

books, magazines
지름의 결과

humidifier
신상

sofa
이사님 침대

camera
캐시백 7만원

book shelf
앙팡이 캣타워

in ma
studio

트라이앵글 페이퍼 3호는
트라이앵글-스튜디오 안의 의미 있는 오브제들을
직접 실크스크린 기법으로 제작한 포스터입니다.

1/100

Indumex

Indumex is a one-stop shop for construction and improvement hardware. Their wide variety of product lines and superior customer service make the shopping experience appealing to every handy-man in the area. The concept was brought to life, intending to portray the brand's values: professionalism and trust. The idea was to convey expertise, without losing approachability. The color palette intends to show contrast, emphasizing Indumex innovation in the market. Blue depicts trust, while orange shows boldness.

Design: Firmalt

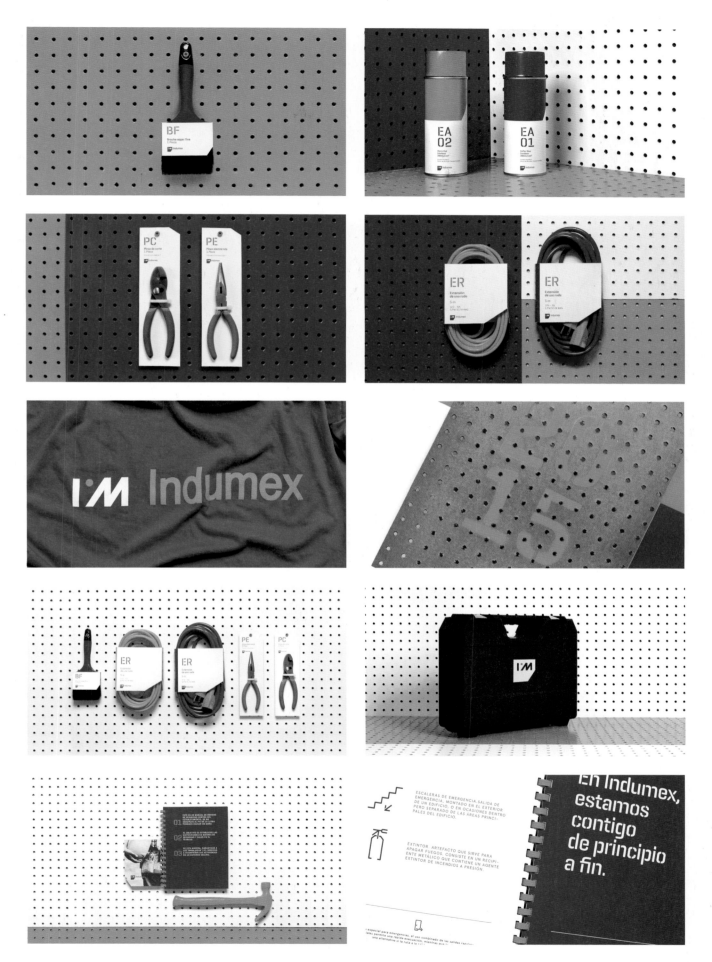

Frenzy Paris

Identity design for Frenzy, a video production company.
For this identity, the design team developed a typeface which expresses a strong personality and elegant effect. Each illustrated animal represents a member of Frenzy. The strong contrast between the energetic red color and the overwhelming blue one enhances the unique personality.

Design: Violaine & Jérémy

Bear Clothing UK

A visual identity for a fashion apparel brand, Bear Clothing UK.
The design was meant to be sophisticated and humorous, in a minimalistic, flat style with the implementation of a bear to suggest the brand name. Different apparel accessory icons such as a hat or a scarf were added to the final version. The color pallet creates a simple yet lively result.

Design: Tiago Machado/Apex Studio

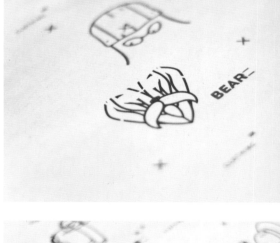
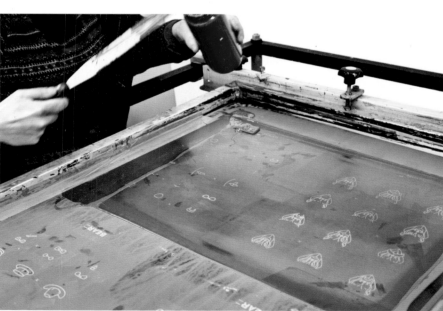
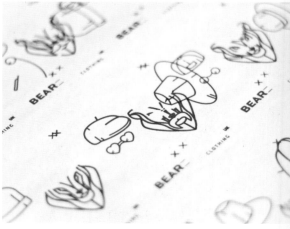

Papa Palheta Brand Experience Kit

The Papa Palheta Experience Kit is designed to reflect their philosophy of having strong coffee roots down in sustainability. In contrast with the earth-tone of the paper stock, the color scheme of florescent orange and cobalt blue provides a pop of color, enlivening the common brown packaging of coffee.

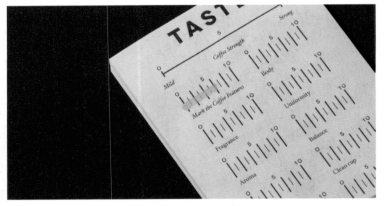

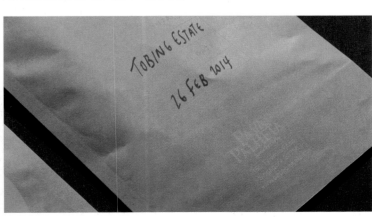

Design: Foreign Policy Design Group

P. S. - Secrets of the Barguzin Skeleton

P. S. is about the story of the greatest Hungarian poet Sandor Petofi's skeleton, which was found in Siberia during an expedition in 1989. The book documents the expedition, provides facts, and was designed to reflect on secrets of the story. Commentary by the author, explanations and annotations of illustration are printed in UV ink, which is only visible under UV light since the designer wants the reader to have the experience of searching for secrets.

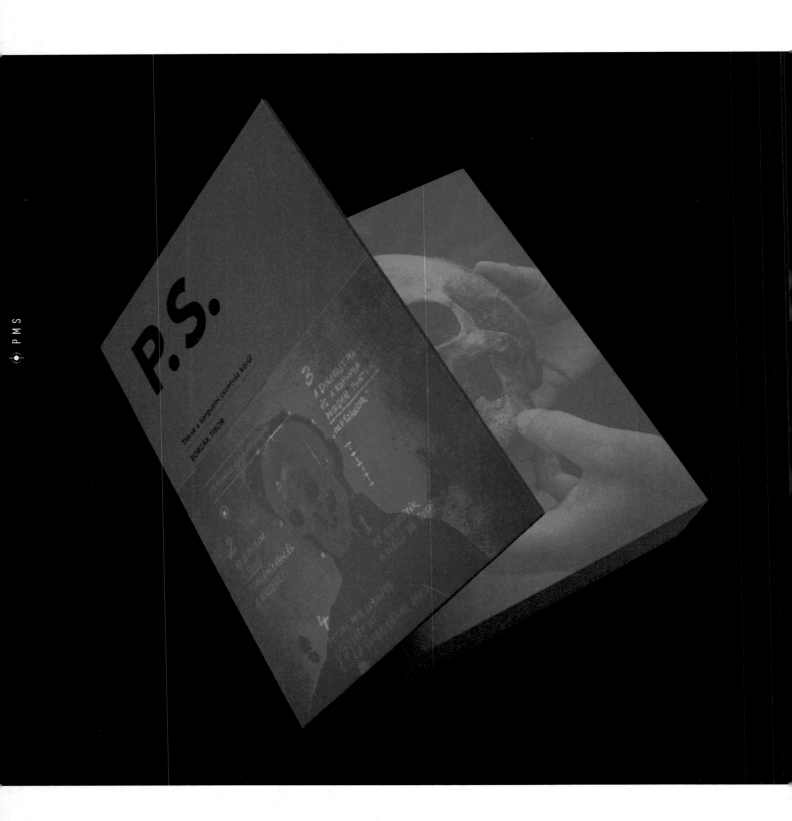

Design: Marton Borzak

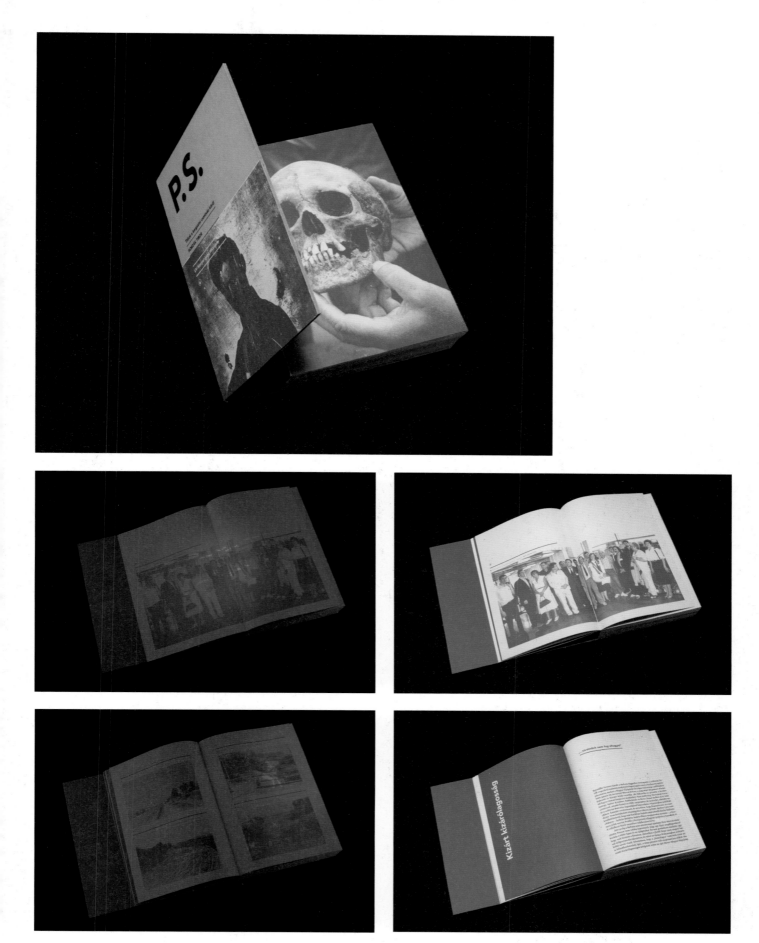

Estúdio Vii Visual Identity

This project presents the development of the visual identity for Estúdio Vii studio. The result is key-low but stunning. The tiny logo is printed consistently on the right side of the kraft paper or white paper. A strong contrast is created and brings viewers' attention to the logo despite its small size. The black graphic pattern on the brown paper adds variations to the whole design.

Design: Eduardo dos Santos / Juliano Simões da Rocha

Le Temps 1998

Visual identity for Le Temps 1998.
Le Temps 1998 is a French bistro based in Taiwan. To fit the bistro's nostalgic style, its stationery design presents the bistro's information and menu on a brown background, creating a harmonious and natural touch.

Design: HOUTH

FEB Design Stationery

This VI for FEB Design studio aimed to show the communicative quality of each one of its materials. The media becomes the message and the central character of this project. The tone of the selected sentences reflects the close relationship between the studio and their clients. By avoiding the use of color, the designers lead all the attention towards the chosen sentences and their message.

P M S

Design: FEB Design & FIBA Design

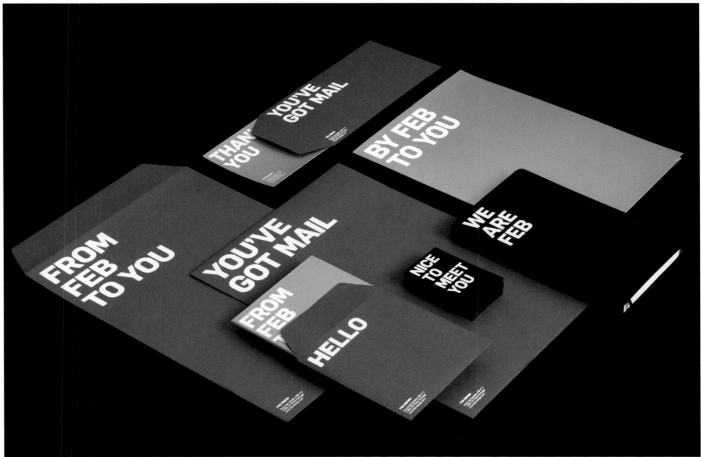

Small Reunions

Packaging design for Small Reunions, a rice brand.
Based on rice grain shape, the patterns for this packaging represent "flowing" images of rice terraces. Each color for each packaging gives a hint to the name of rice grain.

P M S

Design: Shenzhen Pure Life Trading Co.,Ltd

Nördik Impakt: Global Communication

A new identity was designed for Nördik Impakt, an electronic music festival in France. Elegance and quality are the impressions that the design conveys. The bright shades of gold for the poster and the brochure catch the eye with their brilliance.

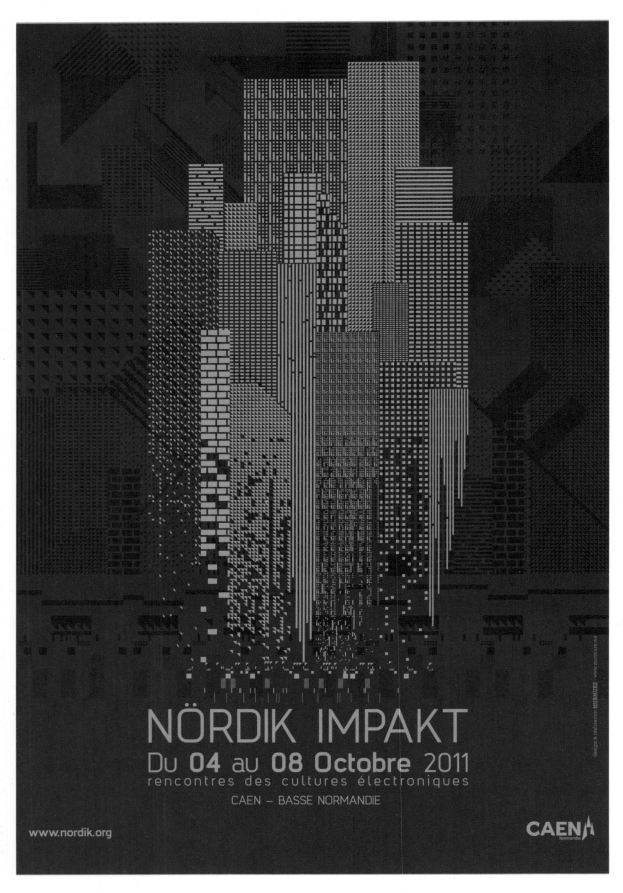

Design: Paul Ressencourt & Julien Alirol / Photo: Murmure

Incognition Business Card

Incognition is a brand consulting agency with a focus on the psychological aspects of branding. On the business card, a brain scan was printed in black on a 380gsm Sirio 80 black card with a spot UV finish on the fracture lines. Against the dark background, the contact info was printed in metallic silver ink.

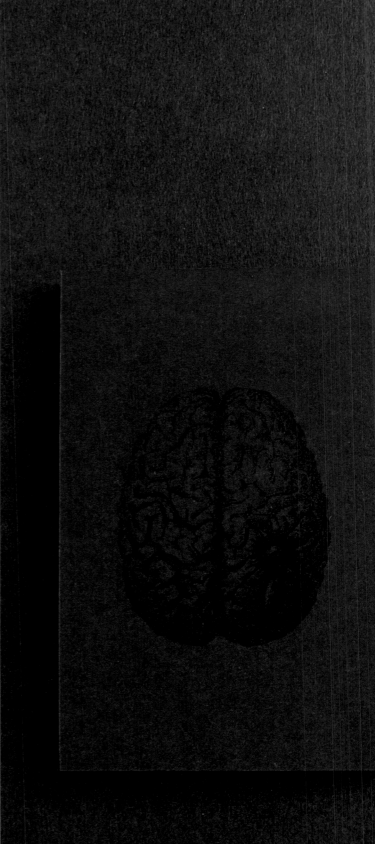

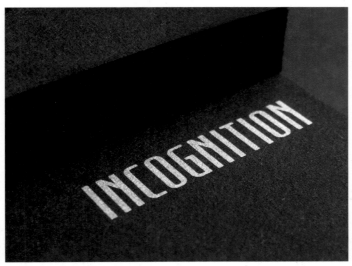

Design: Gene Wang

INCOGNITION

Maurice Quek
Co-founder / Brand Architect

+65 9634 5290
maurice@incognition.co

www.incognition.co

INCOGNITION

Cheong Wei Quan
Co-founder / Brand Engineer

+65 9646 6723
weiquan@incognition.co

www.incognition.co

ACKNOWLEDGEMENTS

We would like to thank all the designers and contributors who have been involved in the production of this book; their contributions have been indispensable to its creation. We would also like to express our gratitude to all the producers for their invaluable opinions and assistance throughout this project. And to the many others whose names are not credited but have made helpful suggestions, we thank you for your continuous support.

FUTURE PARTNERSHIPS:

If you wish to participate in SendPoints' future projects and publications, please send your website or portfolio to editor01@sendpoints.cn.